SPEECHES AND TOASTS

SPEECHES
AND
TOASTS

How to Make and Propose Them

REVISED BY

LESLIE F. STEMP, B.A., LL.B.

BARRISTER-AT-LAW

*INCLUDING
MODEL EXAMPLES FOR
ALL OCCASIONS*

WARD, LOCK & CO., LIMITED

LONDON, MELBOURNE AND JOHANNESBURG

© WARD, LOCK & CO., LIMITED 1959

Entirely New Edition . .	1950
Reprinted	1951
Revised Edition	1952
Reprinted	1954
Reprinted	1957
Reprinted	1959
Reprinted	1962

112

MADE IN GREAT BRITAIN

PRINTED IN GREAT BRITAIN BY
BILLING AND SONS LTD.
GUILDFORD AND LONDON

J2243

PART I

HOW TO PREPARE AND DELIVER THE SPEECH

PART II

SPECIMEN SPEECHES AND TOASTS

8 CONTENTS

PREFACE

A SENSATION of despair, almost of terror, seizes the unfortunate person who feels all eyes turned his way, and hears the cries of **"Speech!"** addressed to *him*—that is, unless he knows **How to Speak!**

Few have the spark of genius that marks the great orator, but, with study and practice, almost anyone can become a convincing and efficient speaker. Command of language, the faculty of presenting thoughts in logical sequence, clearness of utterance, deliberation of manner and earnestness are essential to the speaker.

This book has been written for the would-be speaker who has but little knowledge of how to prepare a speech or how to deliver it when once prepared. In fact, the author has laid himself out to assist the business man or woman, or shall we say "the man in the street," to prepare and make a good speech when called upon to put forward proposals at a company meeting perhaps, or to propose or reply to a toast at some social gathering. First the writer shows how the material for the speech should be collected, arranged, and memorized, he then discusses the pros and cons of speaking from notes only and of carrying the speech written out *in extenso*. Next follow chapters on poise, delivery, elocution and pronunciation. The author has assumed that the reader has had a good grounding in the rules of grammar and he has, therefore, not dealt with its elements, but has given us a most useful chapter called *Errors of the Educated*, in which he has set out many little pitfalls into which we are all liable to fall from time to time. This chapter, together with those on *Style* and *Phraseology*, will enable the speaker to give his speech that little bit of extra polish that turns the rough casting into the finished article.

The Art of Debating has been treated on a generous scale in view of its importance in the training of the speaker; *Extempore Speaking* has also been widely discussed.

Of special interest will be found the regulations for the

formation of and the procedure at Local Parliaments and Debating Societies, and the same may be said of the chapter on
the *Chairman and his Duties*.

In Part II numerous *Model Speeches and Toasts* are given.
It is not intended that they should be learned by heart and
delivered verbatim. Rather are they put forward as outline
drawings from which the beginner may see how to frame the
speech which he may be called upon to make in similar situations. They cover subjects so varied that they may be used
to form the basis of speeches suitable to almost any occasion
and to any audience.

Though the book is primarily written for the tyro, the
writer has treated the subject so comprehensively and has
gone into so much detail that even the man who "rather fancies
his speeches" will find many hints and suggestions well worth
remembering. The book should prove invaluable to Members
of Debating Societies and Local Parliaments, to Chairmen and
Secretaries of Companies and to all Business Men, to Free-
masons, to Civil Officials of all ranks, to After-dinner Speakers
and to all those likely to be called upon to make any pro-
nouncement in public.

THE EDITOR.

WARWICK HOUSE,
116, BAKER STREET,
LONDON, W.I.

PART I

HOW TO PREPARE AND DELIVER THE SPEECH

SPEECHES AND TOASTS

HOW TO MAKE AND PROPOSE THEM

CHAPTER I

HINTS TO SPEAKERS

PUBLIC SPEAKING IN GENERAL

THIS handbook is intended as a guide to those who, at social, public or business meetings, wish to express themselves in a clear and persuasive manner. It is designed to assist those not naturally gifted with the powers of oratory. "Can *anyone* learn to speak?" is a question frequently asked. The following paragraphs will furnish the reply.

With hard work and persistence a measure of success is assured to everyone. Every diligent student can learn to conquer his nervousness and to communicate his thoughts audibly, grammatically and coherently to audiences large or small, and indeed to master all the technique of public speaking. Beyond that everything hangs upon the student's personality. If he is muddle-witted no power can make him argue clearly on the platform, or anywhere else. Speaking is the art of self-expression by means of words, and if the self to be expressed is bumptious, unimaginative and insincere, every one of these vices and defects will be apparent in the speaking. There are fluent speakers who have conquered their own nervousness only to become a source of nervousness to audiences, who are seized with something like a panic when the bore rises complacently "to fill a gap while the more capable orators following me are arranging their thoughts." Out of the abundance of the heart the mouth speaketh. A fluent fool is an offence, but a wise man eloquent is a joy to his fellows. Well, there you have it. If you are a churl you must change your nature if self-expression is to be desirable. That can be done also.

Sincerity and Earnestness.—But if the reader is a good fellow, as we like to believe, he can become a good speaker upon any subject that he has at heart. As to whether any amount of practice will make him an orator—that depends. Oratory implies a touch of genius. Earnestness has this in common with genius—that both are inspirations, but an inspired conscience doesn't produce great works of art (and a fine oration can be classed with these) unless there is also exceptional imagination. Consider, for example, this flight of impassioned oratory taken from a speech delivered in the House of Commons by John Bright shortly after the beginning of the Crimean War:

"The Angel of Death has been abroad throughout the land: you can almost hear the beating of his wings. There is no one, as when the first-born were slain of old, to sprinkle with blood the lintel and the two side posts of our doors that he may spare and pass on."

So strongly did these words appeal to the imagination that many of his hearers looked up, as though to see a visible apparition. A good unimaginative man, however inspired by earnestness, however accomplished in the technique of rhetoric, could not have done that. The visualization of such a tremendous personification could only have been achieved by a man of genius, a maker, a poet.

> "The little more and how much it is!
> The little less and what worlds away!"

Most important is it that the speaker should have clearly outlined in his mind what he is going to say. This seems almost superfluous advice, but it is a fact, as a well-known statesman has reminded us, that there are some speakers who have not the least idea of what they are going to say when they stand up, of what they are saying when they are speaking, or of what they have said when they sit down. It cannot be too definitely laid down that clear thinking is, above all things, essential to clear speaking; ideas cannot be distinctly conveyed to an audience unless the speaker has them ordered and prepared in his mind. Having achieved this he must next strive for clear expression. He must state plain facts, clearly and concisely—call a spade "a spade"—and remember that simplicity of speech obtains immediate approval.

Mere "wordiness" throws too much onus upon the audience,

they have to follow and unravel long and involved sentences and in so doing miss the first half of the speaker's next sentence, and lose the thread of the argument. The good speaker will use short sentences, each composed of a dozen to two dozen words, and varied in length to avoid monotony. A speaker may know his subject thoroughly, but if he uses long and involved sentences his audience will find it hard to arrive at his meaning and the effect will be sacrificed.

Qualifications of a Successful Speaker.—From this it is easy to deduce the qualifications which a speaker must possess to be successful: he must have a command of language with an exact appreciation of the value of words: this he can get by reading; he must have a faculty of presenting his thoughts in logical sequence, so that his arguments are cumulative and in the sum convincing: this he can acquire by writing; he must have clearness of utterance, coupled with deliberation of manner and entire self-possession: this he can acquire by conversation and reading aloud. All these things may be achieved by patient study and intelligent application. The crowning quality which differentiates the supremely great orator from the merely competent one is another matter; it is not to be acquired in the schools; it is the little touch of genius which inspires life into the marble of the sculptor, into the painted canvas of the artist, into the written words of the author, and into the spoken words of the orator; but, although it cannot be taught in the schools, it is bestowed upon the really earnest man much more commonly than is supposed, for something of it is implied in the sincerity of the conviction that compels the individual to give utterance to the thoughts that are in him: inspiration is the word that best describes it.

Earnestness is infectious, and the orator, who at the beginning of his speech convinces his audience that he is himself in earnest, has gone a long way towards gaining their attention and convincing them. The arts which he can acquire by study and by practice will do as much as is humanly possible of the rest. The mysterious power which great orators undoubtedly exercise over their hearers, and which so many people endeavour to explain by such phrases as nerve-force, personal magnetism, and the like, is, if reduced to its simplest terms, little more than the natural result of mere earnestness.

To sum up, it may be said that public speaking is an art that may be easily acquired by all, if they have the will and determination to study and practise and provided they are content to express simple facts in plain, straightforward language. Indeed, in most cases this simple and straightforward manner will appeal to an audience far more strongly than will the rhetoric of a past-master. We say this to encourage those who feel they really have no gift at all for speaking. A surprising number will find, however, that, if they do not possess genius perhaps, they at least have quite a gift for public-speaking.

CHAPTER II

PREPARING THE SPEECH

IT was said long ago that there are only two essentials to good rhetoric; first, have something to say; and next, say it. This short chapter deals with the material, and the next with the delivery of a speech.

Such people as Cabinet Ministers are fortunate in having material of unique interest which all desire to hear, and a thousand listeners are eager for a minute account of their most trivial activities. But to the ordinary speaker material, original in its character and momentous in its import, is not usually available.

Length of the Speech.—Unquestionably the first rule is—Be brief. Your speech will be a failure if the attention of the audience is for one moment allowed to flag: it will never be regained. No exact rule as to time is possible except the quite general one that a speech should be long enough to cover the subject and short enough to be interesting. The second rule is akin to the first—Be relevant. Fix upon your point, make it and leave it. The temptation to wander at large through a mass of superfluities must be rigidly suppressed.

Generally it is wise to be content with one point, because two or more too often tend to counteract each other. If, however, more than one is necessary, the several points should be reduced, as it were, to a common denominator, and utilized as closely related aspects of the same truth.

COLLECTING THE MATERIAL

In collecting the material, first of all give very careful thought to the subject of the speech, remembering always its purpose and aim. Encyclopædias, year-books and other books of reference will furnish information on subjects about which the speaker may not have adequate knowledge. Having studied the matter from every point of view, decide what is the chief aspect you wish to impress upon the audience, for it is better to take one line and work this up thoroughly rather than confront the audience with a mass of unrelated and perhaps irrelevant facts, which they cannot assimilate. Next take a piece of paper, put down this central idea and under it all facts relevant to it. These should now be arranged in order of importance, or more usually in the order in which they will naturally follow, as the thoughts lead from the one to the other. In an argumentative discussion the latter is the better method, as the arguments will then flow smoothly from one into the other and combine to form a complete argumentation.

WRITING OUT THE SPEECH

Having collected your facts and figures, and elaborated your argument, put your notes beneath the blotting pad, and write down the main body of your speech with a full pen, slashing down approximations to figures when you are not sure of them, careless of spelling, grammar and phrasing, employing the first word that presents itself, or leaving a blank if the only possible word eludes you. When you have presented your argument your speech lacks only exordium and peroration to be complete. It still, however, needs revision, polishing, and touching up.

Amplifications and Revisions.—Probably amplifications of your argument will occur to you. Welcome them, but don't let them push the original matter out, even if intrinsically they should be better than some of the passages in the original draft, for *they* have not arisen spontaneously out of the sentences that preceded them as those first sentences did, and it is this spontaneous growth of one idea out of the other that gives life and movement to a composition, and often the best logic.

Because your speech was indited at white heat it is probably stiff with the *clichés* that so easily beset us. Having no time to make phrases of your own it was wise to grasp at these stale, worn-out phrases as stop-gaps. But when you make your maiden speech it must not be cheapened by "slowly but surely's," "not wisely but too well's," "kindly but firmly's," or other *clichés* of this kind.

Do not show off: have your eyes open to detect insincerities of every kind—that Latin quotation dragged in to show an audience who can't understand Latin that you are a classical scholar—that sham self-depreciation which was meant to exalt yourself, anything that tends to keep your personality before the audience. Even an irrelevant anecdote dragged in to get you a laugh is a form of insincerity.

THE PREORATION OR EXORDIUM

Every speech, like every dog, should have a head, a middle, and a tail, or, in more imposing language, preoration, discussion, and peroration. The preoration is most important, as its object is to interest the listeners in the speaker, and should show the "why and wherefore" of the speech. Sometimes the attention of the audience is attracted by the speaker explaining quite shortly the special claims which he has to discuss the particular subject under review. Equally, if not more effective, however, is the sudden discharge of a joke, preferably topical, at the heads of the gathering.

It may consist in the self-introduction of the speaker, a well-turned compliment to the chairman, or a reference to some local achievement. This must be left to the last minute, but the intending speaker should manage to slip away by himself somewhere and write down this semi-impromptu verbatim, because sentences in a conversational vein are harder to memorize than rhetoric, rhetoric like poetry indeed having risen out of the necessity for assisting the memory. Even the speaker who can deliver a memorized speech with confidence should have this conversational exordium written out and should read it. Consisting only of a few sentences, it can be read from the palm of one's hand. This type of exordium, however, has the disadvantage of starting the speech in a key too low, and it is hard, sometimes, to make the necessary key change after the conversational prelude.

Another type of exordium is a striking announcement of the subject. This is much safer for any speaker not very confident of himself. He begins right. Occasionally you hear a double exordium, consisting of a rhetorical plunge into the subject, upon which has been superimposed the conversational exordium prompted by the occasion. This method has great advantages and we wonder, sometimes, why it is not adopted more frequently. Having spoken your few sentences of compliment or graceful banter you then make your true start, assured of not pitching your tone too low.

THE PERORATION OR CONCLUSION

The peroration is, perhaps, the most difficult part of the speech. For the novice in after-dinner speaking it is no doubt safest to call quite simply upon the company to rise and honour the toast, or if responding to a toast to thank those present for the kind way in which they have received it. Sometimes it may be possible to think of an apt quotation which summarizes the conclusions of the speech in striking and memorable language. The accomplished orator will no doubt be able to finish off his oration by a concise summing up, reiterating with renewed emphasis and sincerity his original premises and leading to a mighty climax never to be forgotten by his hearers.

There is possible so much variety in perorations that one has difficulty in beginning to discuss them, and, having begun, even greater difficulty in stopping. There are your poetical perorations, your abrupt, your anecdotal perorations; indeed perorations can take almost any form.

The Poetical Peroration.—Perhaps the finest possible example of the poetical peroration is the conclusion of Joseph Chamberlain's famous speech at Belfast opposing Home Rule —a quotation from Longfellow's "Building of the Ship":

> " 'Thou, too, sail on, O Ship of State!
> Sail on, O Union, strong and great!
> Humanity with all its fears,
> With all the hopes of future years,
> Is hanging breathless on thy fate!' "

Here some of the effect is due to the happy coincidence that Longfellow had employed the word "Union."

When looking around for a stanza to serve as peroration it is worth while to bear in mind the possibility of lighting upon other coincidences not less happy. For this a work of reference such as a good *Dictionary of Quotations* is invaluable. Under the heading of your subject will be, perhaps, scores of poetical passages, one of which will use just the word that brings your audience to its feet as "Union" did Joseph Chamberlain's.

The Climax of the Speech.—A very perfect peroration occurred in a sermon by the Rev. R. J. Campbell upon the Prodigal Son, entitled "The Antiphony of Repentance," and was built up on the repetition of these two sentences: "And the son said, 'Make me as one of thy hired servants.' But the father said, 'Bring forth the best robe and put it on him, and put a ring on his hands.' " When the clock struck the hour at which these Thursday midday services close, Mr. Campbell stopped in the middle of his remarks, and grasping each cover of his Bible, began to bring them together, saying, "And the son said, 'Make me as one of thy hired servants.' But the father said, 'Bring forth a new robe and put it on him, and put a new ring on his hands. For this my son was dead and is alive again, he was lost and is found.'" This was the first time the last text had been included, having been kept back as the final word and summing up. Simultaneously with the enunciation of the word "found" the sides of the Bible met, and the preacher sat down.

Whatever form of peroration you prefer it must be prepared; everyone is agreed upon that—think how disastrous a misquotation would have been to any of the perorations instanced. An incidental advantage is that a prepared peroration gives a speaker confidence to know that an effective close is assured. Finally, it compels him to close at the right moment; no tempting by-way of thought can lure him on to anti-climax.

"FINISHING TOUCHES"

Having erected the framework, it is necessary to give a certain amount of finish to a speech, and a few words may be said regarding the choice of words and the use of humour.

Style.—Many volumes have been written on style. The subject has, however, never been dealt with better than by Aristotle. "Good taste," says that great philosopher, "belongs to that style which is at once full of feeling and clearly descriptive, while the words employed are in proper keeping with the subject-matter. To attain this, the language must be neither tinged with levity in matters of importance, nor lofty on matters that are mean: for if a mean thing is decorated with lofty epithets the result is burlesque." Sentences should be kept short—they are effective and easily understood by the hearers and prevent the inexperienced speaker from becoming involved. Never use words you do not understand, and, above all, *be natural*. Make sure that the construction of your sentences is grammatically correct, for the deliberate delivery necessary to the public speech makes any grammatical mistakes very noticeable.

He who would speak well must observe carefully the speeches of others more experienced than himself, and above all read and re-read the great masters of the English tongue. The exquisite selection of the precisely correct word to apply to each thought is the result of arduous labour and much learning. Much may be done, however, by noting and even memorizing phrases which strike and impress us.

An audience is quickly irritated by the continued repetition of familiar words such as "*good*," "*quite*," "*but*," and especially "*it*." Not only is the last, if oft repeated, ugly, but it also tends to obscure the meaning of a sentence. Every aspirant to public speaking should, by reading good literature and by the use of a trustworthy dictionary, endeavour to improve his vocabulary, so that alternatives to the much-used words will readily come to mind. At the same time avoid trying to be clever, do not use long words unnecessarily, even if you do know the meaning of them; as said before, simplicity of speech is the ideal at which to aim.

As to quotations from other speakers and from the newspapers, these are good up to a point, but if too many are included in a speech the audience will receive the impression that the speaker has but few ideas of his own and must draw upon the brains of others. In a debating speech quote your opponent by all means, and endeavour to show that his arguments are faulty and so score heavily. Poetical quotations are, at times, useful, especially in the peroration, but like all other quoted matter must be used sparingly.

Humour.—Humour is, without doubt, most effective when it is topical, and an opportunity often arises from some incident at the meeting: a play on names or a witty retort to some part of the preceding speech is a device not to be entirely despised. There are some stories, though very few, which are so good that it is permissible to go to a little trouble to bring them in. The ordinary funny story, however, should be rigidly excluded unless it is absolutely relevant and appropriate to the occasion. In telling a story come to the point as soon as possible: it matters little if the man's name was Jones or Smith or whether you witnessed the incident while you were in a car or walking. It is to be remembered that however good your story may be there is certain to be someone who will not find it amusing, and however old it may be someone will not have heard it.

Vulgarity—Slang—Colloquialisms.—Vulgarity will often raise a laugh, but it is the bankruptcy of wit, and the man who laughs most loudly at it is often the severest critic of its author. Some men have that happy art of being able to say the most personal things in a way that will delight and amuse the butt of their wit as well as the whole company. This gift is given by the gods to few indeed, and as a general rule personalities of all kinds should not be used.

Slang and swear-words must be shunned in public speaking, and colloquialisms should normally be avoided, although quite allowable in conversation.

Bearing the above points in mind, the speech should be carefully read over word by word and any adjustments made. The whole speech should then be written out in full, by hand, further to impress it upon the memory. This is excellent training, and every opportunity should be taken to commit the speech to paper until the would-be orator feels that he is " word-perfect."

MEMORIZING THE SPEECH

Well, now, your speech is ready, and your next task is to memorize it. Then comes the rehearsal, in a room by yourself. It will be enough if you say the words below your breath. Carry the speech through to a conclusion of some sort when your memory fails. Don't hark back for a fresh start : you won't be able to do that at the meeting. Having got off the path of your written speech, it is capital practice to force your way through obstructions to rejoin it at some point further on in the argument. You are acquiring resourcefulness.

Timing the Speech.—Time yourself and see how long it takes you to deliver the speech. You can then cut it or add to it so that its delivery will occupy the allotted time.

Above all things, don't rehearse your speech before others. A meeting is much more receptive than an individual, and domestic criticism is rarely helpful, being merely rich in suggestion of deletions. If you rehearse your speech round the family, all that will be left of it will be a few bones.

NOTES AND HEADINGS

Although for constructional purposes and to assist the memory it is best to write the speech out in full, the practice of carrying the written speech in the pocket, unless carefully "headed and noted," is a dangerous one, for the speaker may become flurried and not able to find the exact place at which he has arrived in his document, or he is tempted to read long extracts from his manuscript. Such a course may be disastrous to the effect of his speech. Conversely if no notes are used the novice may become unduly nervous while he is making one point, and in consequence may forget another, or may confuse the due sequence of his argument. The happy medium is the use of headings and sub-headings, which come quickly to the eye and thereby afford a sense of security. These headings must not be allowed to grow into long notes which will be worse than useless, for the speaker will lose himself among them; they will be no better than the complete speech. Notes must be clear and concise and set out so that the speaker can find his place and pick up the threads of his speech at a single glance. As explained above, these headings must be closely co-related and flow easily the one into the other.

As an illustration of the use of notes and headings, let us imagine a chartered accountant proposing the health of the Royal Institute of British Architects. The most useful notes might be somewhat as follows:

NOTES

Preoration.—Castles in the air; often built by architects; demolished by accountants.

Material for Discussion.—Buildings are: (*a*) The best historians. (*b*) Best symbol of national prosperity. (*c*) Best social reformers.

Peroration.—Interdependence of professions. Pay us our fee, and you will never lack purchasers for your beautiful houses.

SPEECH

THE ROYAL INSTITUTE OF BRITISH ARCHITECTS

Proposed by a Chartered Accountant

It is a pleasure to propose the health of this great Institute whose guests we are to-night: and it is especially pleasant to one of my profession thus to prove that Accountants share the gift of speech with other mortals. I can, however, assure you that we have other recreations than taking out trial balance sheets, although it is no doubt necessary that we should sometimes pursue our clients to their castles in the air, and remind them of the more—shall I say—sordid side of life?

The history of a nation is to be read in its architecture, for true art is a mirror in which we can read the moral and intellectual qualities of its creators. The great buildings of cities are imperishable records, reminding us not only of the material prosperity of a nation, but also of the taste and refinement of its people. In this respect, speaking humbly as a layman among many eminent members of your profession, I do not think I need hesitate to say that we have no cause to be ashamed of the legacy we hope to bequeath to our children.

But to-day we are also coming to realize the important part that the science of architecture plays in our national life. We read that it was the lofty temples and vast amphitheatres of Rome that astounded and intimidated our ancient forefathers; and it is no less true that modern Empires have seen the necessity of erecting and maintaining in their capitals buildings proportionate to the majesty of their jurisdiction. The inward and spiritual grace of good and sound government is fostered, if not created, by its outward and visible signs.

To-day our great commercial houses are seeking to symbolize their credit and security in material bricks and stone, and it is gratifying to realize that so much of the beautifying and ennobling of our great cities is due to private enterprise of this kind.

But your profession is also taking a noble part in the work of social amelioration and uplift which is so characteristic of to-day. The great care and attention which you bestow upon the design of private dwellings will, I believe, foster a new spirit of pride and self-respect in our citizens. A new type of domestic architecture has arisen which, whatever hard things may be said of it, appears to me a great improvement on the monotonous rows of ugly villas which disfigure so many of our streets. The compact and labour-saving houses which have been built are a proof, if one were needed, that your profession has its finger on the pulse of the people, and is quick to adapt itself to the social changes of our day. That this is so must be largely due to your Institute, through which the high standard of your membership is maintained, and co-operation within your profession is facilitated.

I am glad that I can proffer my feeble praise without any feeling of disloyalty to my own profession.

All professions are interdependent in these days, and we feel that we take an essential if humble part in the great work you are doing: in fact we feel we do you a double service, for although our fees relieve you of a minute percentage of your millions, we return it to you when we purchase your beautiful houses. Gentlemen, I bid you rise and drink the health of the Royal Institute of British Architects.

Reading the Speech.—The full manuscript may, of course, be carried in addition to the notes if the speaker feels more confident with it in his pocket. Only as a last resort, however, should the speech be read; if this must be done, try to repeat from memory long sentences, especially those forming the climax of an argument. This will make the speech far more telling. Don't read too quickly, nor yet in a dull monotonous sing-song; try to read naturally as if talking, deliberately and slowly. When reading a speech many novices hold their manuscripts up in front of their faces and hide them from the audience, a fatal mistake, as all the personal element is at once banished from the speech: on the other hand, don't attempt to hide your notes; read, where you must read, quite openly: the audience will soon detect any dissembling of this nature. If it is not possible to memorize the whole speech, try at least to get the peroration or conclusion fixed firmly in the memory. It is the straw at which the novice in distress can clutch, for it tells him when and how to finish, sums up the most telling points in the oration and, as a good finish, will often save an otherwise hopeless effort from complete failure.

CHAPTER III

DELIVERY

WITH regard to the actual delivery of a speech, only a few general hints can be given in the limited space available here. There are many books upon elocution to which reference may be profitably made, and it may be said, incidentally, that far too little attention is nowadays paid to elocution.

The Speaker's Position.—The position of the head is of primary importance: it should not be held too high or the muscles of the throat will be restricted; it should, in fact, be tilted slightly forward and downward, and for this reason the speaker is usually placed on a platform from which he may look down upon his audience. The speaker should not commence to speak until he is actually standing upright—few things look more ridiculous or pitiable than the nervous speaker discharging a rapid volley of confused and half-heard words, while still in a semi-crouching position. Once on his feet he should make a momentary pause, face the audience squarely, or the chairman if addressing him, and then, but not before, let him commence his preoration.

In debating speeches or at political meetings many speakers pick out some individual who seems to be especially sceptical, and address themselves to this person, for a time at any rate, and use all their powers to convince him. If he is won over the speaker may be pretty sure that he has swayed the remainder of the audience. The head and shoulders—the legs and feet must not be moved—should from time to time be turned to the left or right so that all parts of the audience may be addressed; they will otherwise feel that they are being neglected. The position of the hands worries most novices. They should not rest upon the table in front of the speaker, as this is usually too low, and most emphatically must the arms not be folded over the chest, as this will impede the breathing. Many speakers grasp the lapels of their coats, but if the back of a chair is handy it will form an ideal support for the hands. Something to grasp seems to give the speaker confidence—never allow the hands to wander about nervously and aimlessly.

Management of the Breath.—Proper management of the breath is the fundamental necessity in the effective use of the voice. For public speaking the important thing is to take in as much breath as possible, inflate the lungs to their fullest extent with air, and never exhaust them. Take fresh breaths whenever and wherever opportunity offers. The shoulders should be kept back and the speaker should stand upright with his chest expanded but more or less inactive, as the breath should be controlled by the muscles below the diaphragm and not by those of the chest itself.

Pronunciation.—Some control of the breath having been acquired, the next point to consider is its application to the vocal organs in producing speech. "Pronunciation" is simply giving utterance to words, and when clearly and effectively done the vocal act is defined as correct articulation: when many words are spoken successively, with due regard to their emphasis and inflexion, the speaker is said to have flexibility of utterance. Words are formed by the action of the tongue, lips, and nose, and consequently the sounds should be articulated by the organs of the mouth, not by those of the throat.

Articulation.—To acquire correct articulation every word should be delivered perfectly finished; neither should words be hurried over and run one into another, nor should they be prolonged or drawled. Especial attention should be given to the due articulation of the final syllables of each word. Too often this is neglected in the case of words ending with "d" and "k" and also in the "g" in the frequent suffix "ing," with the result that the words are "clipped" and the effect is bad. When all the vocal apparatus is subordinated to the will so completely that each organ responds to the production of any tone or variation of sound, "flexibility" has been acquired.

An admirable exercise in articulation has been suggested by one writer on the subject. After describing various exercises, he said: "It would be advantageous to take any piece and read it backwards. I do not know of any practice more likely to produce clear articulation than this. In performing it great care should be taken to let each word stand out, above and apart from its neighbours. It will, also, be necessary that each letter in the syllable and each syllable in the word should be distinctly heard. And here we may lay down a very good rule—let every letter and every syllable be distinctly heard, unless there is some good reason against it. Take care to enunciate each word as loudly as conveniently possible. Breathe between each word. It would be a good practice, and would vary the above, to elongate the syllables as much as possible, and also to read in several keys, or, in other words, with the different kinds of pitch of which the voice is capable."

We quote this because a single experiment will convince any ordinary person that his usual articulation is much more faulty than he would previously have believed, and whatever else a sympathetic audience may forgive in the way of harshness of voice, or stiffness of gesture, they will not overlook failure in articulation. If a speaker will not take the trouble to make every word he says clear, he will forfeit the sympathy, and very speedily the patience, of his hearers.

Further, it should not be forgotten that clear articulation goes a long way to compensate for weakness of voice. Speak at first to those at the back of the hall: if they can hear, all can; if they cannot, either pitch the voice a little higher or speak more deliberately. Once the correct pitch is obtained the speaker need not worry further on this point. Medium pitch is the ideal to aim at; too low a pitch will not carry, while nothing is more irritating to an audience than an excessively high-pitched voice. If the audience are interested at the outset, they bring their eyes as well as their ears into use, and catch every word that is perfectly articulated; no pains, therefore, should be spared to make the articulation precise and accurate.

Tone and "Pitch."—The would-be orator must guard against artificiality of voice, which will place an undue strain upon him and at the same time detract from the atmosphere of sincerity and naturalness which he would desire to convey. The acoustic properties of many halls, especially banqueting halls, are bad; but difficulties of this kind can be overcome best by using the natural voice which the speaker is accustomed to use in everyday conversation. By developing this voice, the high and low pitch are avoided and the temptation to shout is overcome. The true aim should be to give penetrating power to the natural or middle voice by projecting it forward through the teeth, endeavouring at the same time to keep the tone smooth, round, and full.

"Time" and "Vocal Punctuation."—The speaker must further consider the question of "time," the rapidity with which he will give utterance to his words; in this case again he must be guided by the paramount necessity of clear articulation,

with which neither speed nor anything else must be allowed to interfere; something of the "time" will be indicated by the nature of the passage to be spoken, an impassioned appeal or a fiery denunciation demanding greater rapidity than a solemn exhortation or a critical analysis of the arguments of the other side. As a general rule, however, rapidity tends to reduce the apparent importance of the subject matter, while deliberate utterance enhances it and makes for effective speech—but the speaker must not be pompous. He must be sincere, and show that he believes every word he is saying. This earnestness will do more than anything to give him the power of persuasive speech. Finally, he must pay due regard to proper phrasing and grouping of his words : this has been well defined as "vocal punctuation," and consists in arranging the words into groups so as to convey their actual meaning, and in separating them by the use of pauses in utterance. The would-be speaker must avoid also the very common habit of dropping the voice at the end of a sentence, especially as this is often the most important phrase, and will probably be left unheard.

To sum up, anyone with a very little preliminary instruction can learn to control and economize his breath, can acquire clear articulation, and practise effective gesticulation; the rest he can learn best by listening to and watching such good speakers as he may have the opportunity of hearing. By taking pains he may soon hope to become a competent and convincing speaker himself.

THE USE OF THE PAUSE.—A few thoughts about the right use of pauses may prove of value.

A pause must be made after the subject or subjective phrase; e.g.

"Honour—demands the sacrifice."

"The last day of that long year—was drawing to a close."

"Kindness is the golden chain—by which society is bound together."

"Poor, gentle, patient, noble Nell—was dead."

A pause is made after the inverted phrase whenever the form of a sentence is inverted; e.g.

"Few and short—were the prayers we said."

"And ever unto me there cometh—an impulse from the sea."

"With his white hair unbonneted—the stout old sheriff comes."

"O'er Longleat's towers, o'er Cranbourne's oaks—the fiery herald flew."

"Within a windowed niche of that high hall—sat Brunswick's fated chieftain."

Another important pause is that which occurs in every ellipsis; e.g.

"Though deep—yet clear; though gentle—yet not dull; strong—without rage; without o'erflowing—full."

A pause occurs both before and after a prepositional phrase; e.g.

"Once upon a time—of all the good days of the year—upon Christmas Eve—Old Scrooge sat busy in his counting-house."

A pause is made before relative pronouns; e.g.

"He is a freeman—whom the truth makes free."

"They also serve—who only stand and wait."

Pause before and after words in apposition; e.g.

"John of Gaunt—time-honoured Lancaster."

EMPHASIS.—*The would-be speaker's attention must be drawn to the need for proper emphasis of contrasted verbs; e.g.*

"If you *show* mercy you shall also *receive* mercy."

"That which man *has* done, man *can* do."

After laying emphasis upon a thing, when it comes to be mentioned again, move the emphasis on to some word relating to that thing; e.g.

"When I was a *child*, I *spake* as a child, I *understood* as a child, I *thought* as a child."

Words repeated have an increased emphasis; e.g.

"Alone, *alone*; all, *all* alone; *alone* on a wide, *wide* sea."

"Scrooge thought and *thought*, and THOUGHT it over, and *over*, and OVER, and could make nothing of it."

The emphasis of climax comes whenever we have a series of words, and each succeeding word requires a greater stress; e.g.

"While *stands* the Coliseum, *Rome* shall stand; when FALLS the Coliseum, ROME shall fall; and when ROME FALLS— THE WORLD."

CHAPTER IV

PRONUNCIATION

PRONUNCIATION is an important matter, the difference between correct and incorrect pronunciation marking the difference between an educated and an uneducated man. In ordinary conversation the most common errors are due to carelessness, to a slipshod speech, which is tolerated for no apparent reason, and which many parents check in their children only when it degenerates into such glaring faults as omission of the aspirate or its insertion in places where it should not be. In public-speaking, however, correct pronunciation is essential, because failure in this particular exposes the orator to public ridicule.

The rule is that, unless there is some explicit reason to the contrary, every letter and every syllable in a word should be heard, and upon this rule too much insistence cannot be laid, for it is to its breach that all the common errors in speech may be traced. It is unnecessary to refer here to variations in pronunciations so localized as to be known as dialect; outside these altogether there are a few words in the case of which custom justifies alternative pronunciations.

The aspirate is, of course, omitted from *heir, honest, honour, hour,* etc.; however it should not be omitted when it follows the letter *w,* but should be given its due value. *What, when, where,* and *whither* are not the same either in sound or sense as *wot, wen, were,* and *wither*; yet many people make no difference in their pronunciation, although they would never think of pronouncing *who* as if it were the exact equivalent of *woo.* But while in the few cases given above the letter *h* is not sounded, there are no exceptions to the rule that it must never be sounded where it does not exist.

R is another letter that is frequently abused. It should never be sounded where it has no place. Yet this is often done, especially when a word ending with a vowel is followed by one beginning with a vowel: "the *idear* of such a thing" and "I saw *ra* man" are common errors in speech which must be avoided. In what is known as lisping, *w* is sometimes substituted for *r,* so that "around the rugged rocks" becomes "awound the wugged wocks"; this used once to be looked

34

upon as an affectation, but, while it is more strictly speaking an affliction, it is usually a curable one, which can be remedied by care and attention.

A few other cases may be profitably given.

Water is boiled in a kettle, not in a kittle; one gets things from shops, does not git them; and people catch fish, do not ketch them. The vowel is sometimes overlooked altogether, and we hear *bas'n* for *basin*, *pedle* for *pedal*, and *contry* for *contrary*. *G* is often ill-treated, sometimes being clipped, so that going becomes goin, dancing dancin, and the like; sometimes being converted into *k*, so that anything becomes anythink, nothing nothink, and so on. Another fault, more common, perhaps, in singing than in speaking, is the sounding of the letter *n* before giving utterance to vowel sounds; this is due to failure in "attack" and can be overcome by a little watchfulness. In certain words the vowels *i* or *e* become *a* and we hear civil*a*ty, qual*a*ty, and many other equally ugly pronunciations. Pillar and pillow, principle and principal, necks and next differ in sound as they do in sense; and finally, many such words as visible, hypocrisy, gospel, goodness, worship, spirit, certain, patience, and others, are marred by having the *u* sound introduced in place of the vowel sounds proper to them respectively, so that visible becomes visuble, worship worshup, spirit spirut, and so on.

WORDS OFTEN MISPRONOUNCED

Word.	Correct Pronunciation.	Incorrect Pronunciation.
Applicable	A'-pplicable	Applic'-able
Ate	Et	Ate
Brusque	Broosk	Brŭsk
Clerk	Clark	Clurk
Decade	Dĕc'-ade	De-cade'
Dew	Dew	Doo
Diocesan	Di-os'-esan	Dĭ-o-ses'-an
Due	Dew	Doo
Facet	Făs'-et	Fay'-set
Favourite	Fā'-vor-it	Fā-vor-ate'
February	Fĕb'-ru-ary	Fĕb'-u-ary
Fellow	Fellow	Feller
Feminine	Fĕm'-in-in	Fĕm'-in-ain
Gist	Jist	Gist

Word.	Correct Pronunciation.	Incorrect Pronunciation.
Gondola	Gŏn'-dola	Gŏn-dō'-la
Height	Hīt	Hītth
Heinous	Hay'-nus	Hī'-nus or Hī'-nē-us
Incomparable	In-cŏm'-parable	In-cŏm-pair'-able
Institution	Insti-tew'-shon	Insti-too'-shon
Learned (adj.)	Learn'-ed	Learnd
Mausoleum	Mauso-le-um	Mauso'-leum
Mischievous	Mis'-chivus	Mis-chee'-vus
Nothing	Nuthing	Nuthink
Often	Of-en	Of-ten
Opposite	Op'-posit	Oppo-sīte'
Personalty (Personal Property)	Per'-sonalty	Per-son-al'-ity
Politic	Pŏl'-it-ik	Pŏl-it'-ik
Position	Po-zish'on	Per-zish'-on
Potato	Po-tay'-to	Per-tay'-ter
Precedent	Prĕs'-eedent	Pree-see'-dent
Primer (Elementary Book)	Prĭm'er	Prīme'-er
Pronunciation	Pro-nun'-siay-shon	Pro-nown'-siay-shon
Radish	Radish	Redish
Remonstrate	Rem-on'-strate	Rem'-on-strate
Reciprocity	Resi-prŏs'-ity	Resip'-rosity
Secretary	Sek'-retary	Sek'-ertary
Superfluous	Soo-per-floo-us	Sooper-floo'us
Timbre	Tămbr	Tĭmbr
Tuesday	Tews'-day	Toos'-dy
Vagary	Va-gār'y	Va'-gary
Victuals	Vit'-ls	Vik'-tew-als

THE PRONUNCIATION OF DIFFICULT NAMES

Custom changes, spelling exercises a continuous pull, and there is always a tendency for strange pronunciations to lapse into desuetude. This tendency is particularly marked with place names.

A large number of names of musicians have been included in the following list, as these are often a cause of stumbling.

Name.	Pronunciation.	Remarks.
Alnwick	Annick	
Ayscough	Ascoff	First syllable accented
Bach	Barkh	
Banff	Bamf	
Bayreuth	Byroit	
Beaconsfield	Becconsfield	As a place name
	Beaconsfield	As a personal name
Beauchamp	Beecham	
Beaulieu	Bewly	
Beethoven	Bayt-hoven	First syllable accented
Belvoir	Bever	
Berkeley	Barkley	
Bethune	Beetun	
Bicester	Bister	
Blount	Blunt	
Boscawen	Boscawn	
Bromwich	Brumich	
Brough	Bruff	
Buccleuch	Bucklew	Second syllable accented
Burleigh	Burley	
Cadogan	Caddugan	
Cannes	Can	
Cecil	Secil	Not Seecil
Cenci	Chenchy	
Charteris	Charters	
Cholmondeley	Chumly	
Cirencester	Sisister	
Clough	Cluff	
Cockburn	Co-burn	
Colquhoun	Cŏhoon	Second syllable accented
Cowper	Cooper	
Crichton	Cryton	
Derby	Darby	
Disraeli	Dizrayley	Second syllable accented
Donoughmore	Donomore	
Drogheda	Droider	
Duchesne	Doushayn	
Du Plat	Du Plar	
Evelyn	Eavlin	
Farquhar	Farkwar	
Faulk	Fōk	
Fowey	Foy	
Glazounoff	Glarzoonnoff	Second syllable accented
Goethe	Geuter	
Gounod	Gouno	First syllable accented
Gower	Gore	
Hawarden	Harden	

Name.	Pronunciation.	Remarks.
Heine	Hine-er	
Heloise	Heloĕze	Three syllables
Herries	Harris	
Hobart	Hubbert	
Home	Hume	
Irene	Eireenee	Three syllables
Keighley	Kethley	
Kerr	Carr	
Kilmalcolm	Kilmakoam	Third syllable accented
Kirkcudbrightshire	Kerkewbrishire	Second syllable accented
Knollys	Knowles	
Kussevitzsky	Koossayvitskee	Third syllable accented
Launceston	Lawnston	Two syllables
Mackay	McKye	
Mahon	Mayon	
Mainwaring	Mannering	
Marjoribanks	Marshbanks	
McLeod	McCloud	
Menai	Menny	
Menzies	Mingies	
Meux	x sounded	
Millais	Millay	
Millet	Millay	
Molyneux	x sounded	
Mussorgsky	Moossorgskee	Second syllable accented
Pall Mall	Pell Mell	Second word accented
Pavlova	Pahvlovah	First syllable accented
Pepys	Peeps [payee	
Pompeii	Pompeyi or Pam-Tolemey	First syllable accented
Ptolemy		
Quixote	Cwixot or Kihóté	
Rabelais	Rablay	
Rachmaninoff	Rach-ma-ne-noff	Second syllable accented
Raleigh [name	Rawley	
St. John (as a sur-	Sinjin	
St. Leger	Sellinger	
Sandys	Sands	
Scriabin	Scree-arb-in	Accent on arb
Seattle	See-at-l	
Stravinsky	Strah-veenskee	Accent on second syllable
Teignmouth	Tinmuth	
Tschaikovsky	Tchaikovskee	Accent on kov
Tyrwhitt	Tirrit	
Versailles	Vairsigh	
Wagner	Vargner	
Waldegrave	Wallgrove	Two syllables
Wemyss	Weems	

RULES OF PRONUNCIATION

By memorizing general rules like the following we can materially reduce errors in pronunciation: —

Doubled Consonants.

Doubled consonants are generally pronounced as single (*e.g. beginner* as *begin-er*), except in compound words or words with a prefix that can be used separately; *e.g. cutthroat, out-top.*

The letter C.

Before *a, o, u,* or any consonant except *h,* **c** is pronounced hard like *k,* and also when it is the terminal letter of a syllable, unless followed by *e* or *i* in the next syllable; *e.g. calm, cone, cut, climb, romantic, social.*

C is pronounced soft like *s* before *e, i,* or *y; e.g. cell, cigar,* and *cygnet.*

Ch. The usual pronunciation of **ch** is as in *chance*; but in words derived from the Greek it often has the sound of *k,* as in *chasm.* In words derived from French it is often pronounced *sh,* as in *nonchalance.*

The letter G.

G is hard, as in *gate,* when it forms the terminal letter of a word, and in derivatives of words ending in *g; e.g. dig, digger.* This is true almost without exception whether the *g* is doubled or not. It has the hard sound too before *a, o, u, l,* and *r,* when occurring in the same syllable as itself, and before *e* and *i* in words derived from Anglo-Saxon or German; *e.g. gate, goat, gut, glance, grand, gelding,* and *gilt.*

G is pronounced soft (as *j*) before *e, i* or *y* in words derived directly or indirectly from Latin, except when *g* is doubled before *y,* or the word is a derivative of one ending in *g,* when the rule given above is followed; *e.g. general, gentle, margin, gypsum.*

The letters PH.

The usual sound of **ph** is like *f,* as in *photo.* Sometimes, as in *naphtha,* the *ph* is given the sound of *p*; but even the *f* sound is not wrong, and indeed is even preferred by some authorities. In a very few words, *ph* is pronounced *v*.

The letters S and SS.

The usual pronunciation of *s* is as in *sand*. When the *s* is doubled it is pronounced as a single *s*. When preceded by a vowel at the end of an accented syllable *s* is pronounced *z* before *i* or *y*; *e.g. erosion*. *-Sion* is pronounced usually *-shon*; *e.g. session, mission. S*, as the final sound of a word, is often pronounced like *z* when we *use* (*uze*) the word as a verb, but as *s* (sharp) when we make *use* (*use*) of it as a noun.

The syllables -tion and -tial.

Almost invariably *-tion* is pronounced *-shon* and *-tial* as *shal*.

The letter Y.

An unaccented *y*, when terminating a word, is always sounded like a short *i*, as in *him*, but if accented is long like the *i* in *time*.

CHAPTER V

ERRORS OF THE EDUCATED

GRAMMATICAL MISTAKES ALL ARE APT TO MAKE

IN this chapter we consider certain besetting carelessnesses of dictum from which even our high-brows are not immune. Errors of speech that arise from ignorance of the laws of grammar are not here discussed, as it has been presumed that readers have had a good grounding in elementary grammar.

"That" and "Which"

It is wrong to use the relative pronouns "that" and "which" as if they were interchangeable, and to be varied to meet the demands of euphony. Their provinces are distinct; the boundaries between them well marked. Every defining clause whose antecedent is not a person should be introduced by *that*, every such clause that adds new matter by *which*. The test of defining clauses is : would the suppression of them render the statement untrue? If so it is a defining clause. "We have rejected all the cases that arrived sea-damaged." Omit the clause and what remains is a falsehood : *all* the cases were not rejected : the sound were accepted. "We have received your statement, which is receiving our attention." Even if this sentence were cut short after "statement," it would be true. The first sentence, therefore, contained a *defining* clause, properly introduced by "that," and the second an added clause, preceded, correctly, by "which."

"And Which"

"Which" itself can mean "and this." Therefore "and which" is to be avoided except where unescapable, as in : "He gave me a bat, which I accepted gratefully, and which exactly suited me." Delete the second "which" and the first would be at once the accusative of the verb "gave" and the nominative of "suited," and, grammatically, this must not be. The second "which," therefore, is necessary and it can be introduced in no other way than by "and."

"That" and "Who"

There is little room for mistake in usage here, because where uncertainty exists either is correct, but this very fact occasions much mistaken criticism. Originally "that" sponsored *all* defining clauses whether the antecedent were a personal noun or not. Shakespeare wrote: "The man that hath no music in his soul," and this is still the practice of many careful writers. The general opinion is that this use of "that" has become archaic, and "who" is now preferable, but superlatives demand the older form: "Jones is the best batsman that the club has ever had."

Possessives

Personal nouns form the possessive by adding an apostrophe followed by "s" to the singular; to the plural an apostrophe only, whether the terminal letter of the word itself be "s" or not. Thus we must say "St. James's," but "the Smiths' dance." Euphony is responsible for certain exceptions to the rule for double "s" in the singular. When the last syllable begins with the letter "s" or is immediately preceded by "s" the final "s" is not doubled; thus: "Moses' visit to the fair," not Moses's. Similarly with Greek proper nouns, particularly long names, Archimedes for example, but the exceptions are infrequent in ordinary writing or speech. There are no exceptions to the rule of single "s" with plurals, and the violation of it is a solecism, which the breaking of the other rule is not. "The Smiths's dance" might get a man blackballed at a club, whereas "St. James' " would not cause the elevation of a single critical eyebrow.

Neuter nouns form their possessives differently, as: "the binding of the book." We *shouldn't* say "the book's binding," but often we do.

Gerunds and Active Participles

Good writers sometimes hesitate between "you" and "your" in such a sentence as "I hope to hear of your visiting the invalid." The answer can readily be found by mentally substituting a noun for the gerund and seeing what pronoun the noun would demand, which will be correct also for the gerund. Because you can't say "I hope to hear of you visit to the in-

valid," you mustn't say "you visiting." A handy rule for distinguishing between gerunds and active participles is that with
participles no alternative pronoun is conceivable. "I saw you
fishing." "Your" is out of the question. Therefore where any
uncertainty exists a gerund is present, and gerunds take the
possessive pronoun. When in doubt use the possessive pronoun and you will be right invariably.

UNRELATED PARTICIPLES

The mention of active participles suggests our old friend the
unrelated participle. "Entering the field it was evident that the
home team was losing." Who was entering the field? We must
be told.

SPLIT INFINITIVES

No blunder to-day is more sweepingly condemned than the
split infinitive, but very few critics seem to understand what
constitutes one. They see red about "to immediately go," which
is a split infinitive, an adverb dividing the parts of the verb "to
go"; and about "to be greatly annoyed," which certainly isn't,
there being no verb "to be annoyed." The first should be
altered to "immediately to go" or to "to go immediately," but
the second is correct as it stands, and if changed to "greatly
to be annoyed" would be a thing of scorn to real grammarians.
To escape the dilemma of having to choose between incurring
the wrath of the half-informed and the ridicule of the wise, sub-
stitute an adjective for the passive participle and write "very
angry."

"SHALL" AND "WILL"

The confusion of shall and will, being a Scotticism, is pre-
eminently an error that an educated person might make. The
verb *shall* should be used to express futurity; when intention
only and not futurity is implied *will* must be employed. The
Scots know the rule, accept it theoretically, although in practice they are apt to follow what must be an older orthodoxy in
their country. J. M. Barrie in *When a Man's Single* chaffs his
countrymen about this, making a Scots journalist reply to his
editor, who had asked him if he expected ever to get right with
his future tenses, "I don't think I ever will."

Very little trouble is taken to avoid an error which carries
with it no disparaging suggestion, and even to English ears has

only pleasant associations with holidays in the North, but it can be a real cause of misunderstanding when the speaker expresses futurity in terms that grammatically involve intention.

ADVERBS FOR ADJECTIVES

It being a common error of the illiterate to employ adjectives where adverbs are needed, careful speakers sometimes go to the opposite extreme and use adverbs where they should use adjectives, when some confusing idiom misleads them. "The tea tastes nice." At first glance this seems wrong. "Nice" appears to qualify "tastes," and if so is an adverb and should be "nicely." But does it qualify "tastes"? Is the meaning that the act of tasting is being done well, or is it that the tea itself is nice? Obviously the latter. The idiom is a contraction of "the tea tastes to be nice." A tea-taster tastes nicely (or carefully) and, as a result, the teas he blends taste nice.

THE NOUN CLAUSE

The error here is to treat a single word as the object of the verb that governs the whole clause: "I know whom that girl is." Logic should make this impossible. You don't know the girl, but only her identity, who she is. The object of the verb is the whole noun clause, each separate word of which must be written as if the clause were an independent sentence. "Whom do you think will win?" is, perhaps, a more representative example of this mistake.

WRONG BY CHOICE

Authors will often allow a grammatical error to remain when the correction of it would involve awkwardness. The law of elision, that a verb cannot be dropped unless there is left in charge another verb of the same number, is often thus defied. "His face was badly frozen and his ears, hands and feet." If such a sentence be challenged by a proof-reader or sub-editor the author will withstand him on the ground that the insertion of the second verb would spoil the sentence. Then recast it. The dilemma arises almost invariably in the patching of loose constructions. Writers whose grammar is impeccable never seem to have any difficulty in avoiding unnaturalness.

Many sin with their eyes open in the use of "every" and "none," following them by a plural verb, which they know is forbidden, to avoid the otherwise inevitable "he and she," as "Everyone must do what they can" in preference to "he or she can." But there is ample warrant for using the masculine as the common gender. If the context makes this impossible, and you can't say "what he can," drop the "everyone" and say "All must do what they can." Our language badly needs a third person singular that means specifically "he or she."

OVER-NICETY

At the opposite pole to the failing we have just considered is that of over-scrupulousness. The over-nice are capable of "than who." When a usage is universal and has, moreover, the sanction of our greatest stylists from Milton downwards, resistance is futile. "Than whom" is good English and "than who" isn't, or only good school-marm English, another thing altogether. Of course "than" isn't a preposition and shouldn't govern a relative in the accusative, but it does, and that is all that can be said about it. Explaining that "than" used to be a preposition or to have prepositional use doesn't really help, because if that were all the answer would be that we must be guided by what words are to-day. Custom rules, and its decree is "than whom."

Another illogicality that we must accept is "can help" in such a sentence as: "Don't make more grammatical blunders than you can help." Sense demands "can't help." The only blunders to be made are those you can't help making, but sense must bow to custom.

CHAPTER VI

PHRASEOLOGY

PHRASEOLOGY suffers when we employ words that are weak intrinsically, or good words amiss. The misuse of words is so much more culpable that we shall merely glance at the lesser fault.

Words are wrongly constructed when, like *scientist*, they are derived in one part from Latin and the other part from Greek. If you are sufficient of a classic to be able to spot these mongrels, chase them from your speeches! Otherwise don't trouble. Wrongly constructed adjectives are those ending in "able" that are formed from intransitive verbs. *Likeable* is correct—you can like a person—*reliable* is wrong; you can't rely anyone. Logically the word should be *relyuponable*. Instead of *reliable* write *trustworthy*. Brand-new words that merely duplicate existing words are nearly always inferior, as: *happening* for *event*, *lengthy* for *long*, *meticulous* for *extreme* except where trembling solicitude is meant. If *lengthy* why not *strengthy*?

GOOD WORDS MISUSED

Mutual is rightly used in *mutual service*, but wrongly in *mutual friend*. The latter should be *common*.

Like cannot be used with verbs. You are like your father, but you walk *as* he does. Only rustics end sentences with a superfluous "like": "he was quite mazed, like."

Sooner isn't a right synonym for *rather*. "I would *rather* be a door-keeper in the house of the Lord" is English.

Individual as a noun is permissible only when used in opposition to such words as *Government, Committee, Society*, etc.: "A great corporation can take a risk that an individual dare not." In other instances write *person*. "A ragged *individual*" is wrong.

Perspicuous means clear to the understanding. A man is *perspicacious*.

Persons can be *big*, things *large*. You must not tell a young mother that her baby is *large*.

Expect cannot be used about action that is past. It is absurd to say: "I *expect* the cave man must often have gone hungry." The poor fellow has been dead ten thousand years.

Vicarious and *sympathetic* are not synonyms. If you suffer with your friend, your grief is sympathetic; it becomes *vicarious* only when you suffer instead of him. Hence *vicarious* punishment.

Eke out is correct when it means supplement with difficulty, *e.g.*: "My present supply eked out with the ten cases now en route to me." But it is wrongly used in: "With my present supply I will eke out the demands of my summer trade."

MISCELLANEOUS MISTAKES

In each case the wrong word is in italics and the correct word is placed in parentheses after the sentence:

"They divided the apples *between* the three." (among) [*Among* is used when speaking of three or more persons or things; *between* when referring to two.]

"That is not *as* large as mine." (so)

"That is a *very unique* picture." (unique)

"He seldom or *ever* comes to see me." (never)

"You are stronger than *me*." (I) [*E.g.*: "than I am."]

"I spoke to the *Rev. Smith*." (Rev. Mr. Smith)

"It was none other *but* my father." (than)

"It gives me *lots of* pleasure." (much)

"I saw him *previous* to the wedding." (previously)

"From *now on* you must fight for yourself." (this time forward)

"I hate *those kind of things*." (that kind of thing)

"I will tell you some time or *another*." (other)

"I spoke to him at Christmas, since *when* I have not seen him." (which time)

"You can't reach it *without* you stand on a chair." (unless)

"*Less* people were present." (Fewer)

"He has no *less* than six horses." (fewer)

"I cannot speak to him but *what* he is rude to me." (that)

"A hundred pounds *are* not to be despised." (is)

CONFUSION OF WORDS OF SIMILAR SOUND AND SPELLING BUT DIFFERENT IN MEANING

In the English language many words are very similar in sound and form, but may differ greatly in meaning. Care must, therefore, be taken not to misuse words of this kind. A selection of the more common of these is included in the following list, and should be carefully studied.

Anti (pref.), against.

Ante (pref.), before.

Beside, *prep.*, at the side.

Besides, *adv.* or *c.*, over and above.

Bogey, *n.*, fixed number of strokes in golf.

⎰ **Bogy,** *n.*, goblin.   [carriage.
⎱ **Bogie,** *n.*, a railway under-

Born, *p.pt.*, brought forth (child).

Borne, *p.pt.*, carried; endured.

Calendar, *n.*, almanac.

Calender, *n.* and *v.*, press with heated rollers.

Canon, *n.*, regulation; Church dignitary

Cannon, *n.*, great gun; (billiards) hitting of opponent's ball and red ball by cue ball in one stroke.

Canvas, *n.*, sail cloth.

Canvass, *v.*, solicit votes.

Capitol, *n.*, name of a Roman temple.

Capital, *n.*, stock-in-trade; chief city.

Censor, *n.*, critic.

⎰ **Censer,** *n.*, vessel for burning incense.
⎟ **Censure,** *n.*, blame; *v.*, reprove.
⎱ **Census,** *n.*, enumeration of population.

Compliment, *n.*, praise; *v.*, congratulate.

Complement, *n.*, full number.

Contemptuous, *a.*, showing contempt.

Contemptible, *a.*, mean; despicable.

Contiguous, *a.*, touching; neighbouring.

Contagious, *a.*, communicable by touch.

Corporal, *n.*, N.C.O. in Army.

Corporeal, *a.*, having a body.

Courier, *n.*, messenger sent in haste.

Currier, *n.*, dresser of leather.

Dependant, *n.*, one depending on.

Dependent, *a.*, depending on.

Depository, *n.*, storehouse.

Depositary, *n.*, one with whom something is stored.

Desert′, *n.*, merit; *v.*, forsake.

Des′ert, *n.*, sandy plain; *a.*, empty.

Dessert, *n.*, fruit after a meal.

Draught, *n.*, rush of air; liquor drunk at once; plan.

Draft, *n.*, plan; money order; *v.*, draw; detach.

Effect, *n.*, result; *v.*, produce; accomplish.

Affect, *v.*, touch feelings of; act upon; pretend.

Envelope′, *n.*, wrapper; cover.

Envel′op, *v.*, cover; wrap; hide.

Errant, *a.*, wandering.

Errand, *n.*, message.

Except, *v.*, pass over; exclude: *prep.*, without.

Accept, *v.*, take; agree to.

Exec′utor, *n.*, person appointed to carry out will.

Ex′ecutor, *n.*, one who executes.

Fermentation, *n.*, process of fermenting.

Fomentation, *n.*, application of warmth.

CONFUSION OF WORDS OF SIMILAR SOUND AND SPELLING BUT DIFFERENT IN MEANING *(continued)*

Forbear, *v.,* refrain from.

Forbear,
Forebear, } *n.,* an ancestor.

Fungus, *n.,* order of plants of sudden, spongy growth.

{ **Fungous,** *a.,* relating to fungus.
{ **Fungoid,** *a.,* like fungus.

Gauge, *n.* or *v.,* measure.

Gage, *n.* or *v.,* pledge.

Genius, *n.,* spirit; ability; very clever person.

Genus, *n.,* kind; group.

Gentle, *a.,* mild, amiable.

Genteel, *a.,* polite; well-bred.

Gentile, *n.,* one not a Jew.

Imminent, *a.,* impending.

Eminent, *a.,* exalted.

Immigrate, *v.,* come into a country.

Emigrate, *v.,* go from one country to another.

Incredulous, *a.,* unbelieving.

Incredible, *a.,* not to be believed.

Ingenuous, *a.,* open; candid.

Ingenious, *a.,* skilful.

In'valid, *n.,* sick person.

Inval'id, *a.,* of no force; null.

Irruption, *n.,* sudden invasion.

Eruption, *n.,* breaking out.

Licence, *n.,* leave; warrant.

License, *v.,* give authority.

Liniment, *n.,* a soft ointment.

Lineament, *n.,* feature.

Loath, *a.,* unwilling.

Loathe, *v.,* dislike greatly.

Mettle, *n.,* courage; spirit.

Metal, *n.,* gold silver, copper, iron, etc.

Mucus, *n.,* slimy fluid from nose, etc.

Mucous, *a.,* relating to mucus.

Observance, *n.,* act of observing a custom; ceremony.

Observation, *n.,* remark; notice; act of seeing.

Opposite, *a.,* facing; contrary.

Apposite, *a.,* suitable; fit.

Ordnance, *n.,* military stores.

Ordinance, *n.,* regulation.

Pendant, *n.,* jewel; flag; electrolier.

Pendent, *a.,* hanging.

Precede, *v.,* go before.

Proceed, *v.,* advance.

Practise, *v.,* do frequently.

Practice, *n.,* use; habit.

Principal, *n.,* chief man; money at interest: *a.,* chief.

Principle, *n.,* fundamental truth.

Prophecy, *n.,* prediction.

Prophesy, *v.,* foretell events.

Purpose, *n.,* design; *v.,* resolve.

Propose, *v.,* bring forward.

Relict, *n.,* widow.

Relic, *n.,* anything remaining.

Salvage, *n.,* pay for saving goods; goods saved.

Selvedge, } *n.,* natural unfrayable
Selvage, } edge of cloth.

Sew, *v.,* join with thread.

Sow, *v.,* spread seed.

Stationary, *a.,* fixed.

Stationery, *n.,* paper, pens, etc.

Statute, *n.,* law enacted.

Statue, *n.,* image carved from stone, etc.

Stature, *n.,* height.

Status, *n.,* state or condition, rank.

Successive, *a.,* running; following in succession.

Successful, *a.,* prosperous.

Summon, *v.,* call; convoke.

Summons, *n.* or *v.,* call to appear in court.

4

CONFUSION OF WORDS OF SIMILAR SOUND AND SPELLING
BUT DIFFERENT IN MEANING (*continued*)

Tract, *n.,* short treatise. **Track,** *n.,* course; *v.,* trace.
Venal, *a.,* that may be bought. **Venial,** *a.,* pardonable.

REDUNDANCY

In the following list the words in italics are redundant and should be omitted.

Another *one*.
Combine *together*.
Converse *together*.
Decline *to accept*.
Equally *as well*.
Great *big*.
Join *together*.
Rational senses.

Repeat *again* (when one repetition only is meant).
Return *back*.
Very honest.
Very unique.
Very wrong.
Where are you going *to*?

CHAPTER VII

AFTER-DINNER SPEAKING

THE man who is called upon to make an after-dinner speech is more likely to be unaccustomed to public speaking than one who has to address any other gathering. It is very necessary, therefore, that he should endeavour to overcome any natural nervousness he may feel, and at least refrain from shuffling his feet and gazing at the floor or roof, which are its outward and visible signs. He must not be "put off" by the distracting noise of plate or glass or even of whispered private conversation. A little attention to the rules on breathing already outlined will keep the voice steady: and the feeling of nervousness is often defeated by the thought that he is not called upon to say anything novel or dramatic, but merely to express his thoughts, which are almost certainly similar to those of his neighbours. The nearer his remarks approach the general sentiment of the gathering, the better will his hearers be pleased.

The gaze of the audience should not be avoided, but the speaker should look his fellow-guests straight in the face. In argumentative or persuasive speech it is not a bad thing for the speaker to fix upon one person who looks the most unsympathetic or hostile man in the room and to use all his efforts to convince him. Having gained his assent it may be fairly assumed that he has obtained the approval of the majority of his audience. This method is frequently employed by barristers in addressing juries: an individual is selected for particular attention either because he is thought to possess a strong character liable to influence his colleagues, or because he appears to be specially hostile. In a large meeting it is well to select a man well back in the hall: he can then be used as a test of the penetrative qualities of the voice. The after-dinner speaker should, of course, address his remarks to the Chairman.

The manner of making the speech has already been described in the chapter on delivery. A special word may be said, however, about the avoidance of punctuating phrases with a series of "um's" and "ah's." It is fatally easy to do this, and if you begin by falling into the error you will find it will quickly develop into a habit that is very difficult to eradicate. The trouble is that the speaker himself is rarely conscious of how irritating it is to his audience. It completely ruins a delivery that might otherwise be graceful. The fault can be cured only by intensive practice and concentration of will power.

Although it is obviously impossible to deal with all the multitudinous topics which may form the subjects of after-dinner speeches, a few words may be said with regard to the more usual.

The Chief Toasts.—The toast list invariably is headed with the toast of the Queen, and here no speech is required. The Chairman simply utters the time-honoured formula, "Gentlemen, the Queen." While the wording is simple, however, the delivery is important and calls for a good deal of care. The toast should be given with dignity but without exaggerated gravity; the Chairman should aim at being neither too ponderous nor too casual.

The second loyal toast is to the Royal Family. Again no speech is required, but the wording of this toast is naturally variable. A note about this will be found on page 95. This toast is, of course, given only rarely in comparison with the toast to the Queen.

There are other toasts of National scope such as: the Services; Her Majesty's Judges or Ministers; the Bishops and Clergy of all denominations; but these, nowadays, are proposed only at public dinners of first-rate importance, when both proposers and responders will be practised speakers who need no coaching in these or any other points. The man in the street who buys "Speeches and Toasts" and to whose needs the specimen speeches *should* be adapted, may go through life without ever hearing one of these toasts proposed, and doubtless will go through life without himself ever being asked to propose one.

It being our aim to make every page of this book vital and useful, we have limited the specimen examples of these toasts of National scope to the bare minimum necessary to make the book representative, and have thus been able to devote more space to speeches and toasts which the learner, the novice and the aspirant may be called upon to make, propose or respond to.

At annual dinners the toast of the evening is the institution, the regiment, or the firm concerned, and the speech delivered in proposing the toast should always be planned upon a scale commensurate with the importance of the subject; it may refer to the history of the institution, to the place it occupies in the social system, to its method of administration, or to several other aspects of the subject. At dinners given in honour of some particular person, the toast of the evening is "Our Guest," and the speech will, of course, be essentially eulogistic, referring primarily to the events which have directly led to the payment of such a compliment as a dinner in his honour, and, secondarily, to the general career of the guest thus distinguished. In all these cases the speech must be carefully considered and deliberately delivered, for while there is no reason why it should not be happily phrased, and every reason why it should not be heavy, it is intended, primarily, to pay a tribute to the person honoured, and not primarily to entertain or amuse the general company; but always be careful that praise does not degenerate into mere flattery, which will be both absurd and displeasing to the subject of it.

Purely social toasts, such as those generally proposed at sporting dinners, at weddings, and similar occasions, lend themselves to different treatment, and should aim at being light and entertaining.

The Reply to the Toast.—What has been said of speeches delivered in proposing these toasts applies, with the necessary modifications, to speeches delivered in response. The art of after-dinner speaking lies principally in adapting one's remarks to the audience, remembering always that there is less formality at a dinner than on other occasions and that the best after-dinner speakers avoid being too serious.

Points of the After-Dinner Speech.—Dr. Lee, of Johns Hopkins University, in his work, "Principles of Public Speaking," deals with the after-dinner speech, and enumerates the few definite characteristics it should possess.

"First," he says, "it should be brief. Whatever points it makes must glitter like steel and sparkle like the diamond. Wit is also essential, and pathos and fancy should have a place in the scheme. In short, the after-dinner speech, requiring ten minutes for delivery, needs as careful preparation as the expository address that is designed to occupy an hour in utterance. Nothing should be left to the inspiration of the moment, for the chances are that the banquet room will not have a peg upon which to hang an idea. Not only should the theme be discreetly chosen, but it should be thought out and elaborated until every sentence is clear, and the turn of every word provided for. Let nothing be neglected. Even the anecdotes to be related should be put into the choicest language, and when the speaker begins he should have about him the self-consciousness of ready utterance."

Probably this is as good a description of what such a speech should be as can be given in the space of a paragraph. With regard to the question of preparation, the general opinion will probably be in favour of Dr. Lee's assertion that little should be left to the inspiration of the moment, for the number of speakers who can rely upon finding the happy thought and the apt phrase at the critical moment is not large. But, however careful the preparation may be, there are occasions when it will prove to have been wasted. It not infrequently happens that two, or even three, speakers are called upon to respond to a given toast, and many people must have had the tantalizing experience of finding their choicest ideas, and even their happiest phrases, anticipated. In such a case they must trust to their native wit and readiness to save the situation.

Frank confession of the fact that the speaker has been anticipated, made in a humorous manner, has before now met with the best sort of reception, and a good memory for anecdotes is an invaluable possession.

Good humour, tact, and a delicacy of feeling that makes one aware instinctively of the general susceptibilities of one's audience, are perhaps the other attributes that go to make a good after-dinner speaker.

In the following pages will be found speeches and toasts suitable for all sorts of occasions; it must be remembered that they are put forward only as outline drawings, from which the beginner may see how to frame the speech which he may be called upon to make in similar situations; it is not intended that they should be learned by heart and delivered textually; but, properly studied, they may be profitably used as the basis for original orations; at any rate, no one who has so studied them need be quite at a loss for something to say, however suddenly and unexpectedly he may be called upon to propose a toast or make a speech in reply.

Finally, it is strongly recommended that the speaker should

form his own collection of anecdotes, humorous or otherwise, avoiding, of course, the obvious "chestnut." Nothing contributes more to the success of an after-dinner speech than an apposite anecdote well told and well introduced, though of course great care should be exercised in selecting one suitable to the occasion. The introduction of an anecdote at any stage of the speech may be hateful, nugatory or admirable. If possible it should appear to be welded to the rest of the speech and should never appear to have been "dragged in." All anecdotes are ornaments: some are like bangles "that can be slipped on and off," others are like brooches that, sparkling themselves, hold other things together. These are really the only anecdotes worth while.

CHAPTER VIII

THE CHAIRMAN AND HIS DUTIES

A CHAIRMAN is invariably appointed at public meetings, and in all social gatherings of a more or less formal character where speaking is expected. His duties, in the first instance, at public meetings will be briefly considered.

THE CHOICE OF A CHAIRMAN

There may be some difficulty in the appointment of a chairman, and much will depend upon the choice. The person must be intelligent, ready in speech and decision, and capable of enforcing order and making the chair respected by all. He should be a strong man, for chaos is inevitable when the chair is occupied by a weak man whose authority can be brushed aside at any moment by a vigorous and pertinacious mind among the audience.

When the meeting has assembled, the first business is the appointment of a chairman. It happens generally that the conveners of the meeting come prepared to nominate a suitable man as chairman. But one present may propose another, as several others may; and then the question may have to be decided by show of hands. Some of the proposed candidates may not find seconders, which promptly disposes of *them*. These remarks, of course, apply only to occasions where there is present no chairman *ex officio*.

DUTIES OF A CHAIRMAN

The first duty of the chairman is to state clearly and distinctly the objects for which the meeting has been called, or, if there has been a previous meeting, to have the minutes of the proceedings of the previous meeting read. It is then formally moved, "That the minutes be approved," and when this has been carried he signs them.

He will probably read the notice convening the meeting, and proceed to state briefly his views upon the subject in his opening speech. The company will then know enough of the whole matter to be able to take part in the discussion. If the meeting is a political one, he will introduce the chief speaker, remembering that in most cases brevity is an admirable quality in a chairman. On such occasions there will only rarely be any discussion after the main speech; nothing more than the proposal and seconding of a vote of thanks, followed by a reply from the speaker of the evening, and the chairman will call in turn for the proposer and seconder, who will have been chosen beforehand. But on ordinary occasions—on a public platform or the arena of the Debating Society—the chairman will call on some speaker by name—a matter previously arranged—and a seconder having been found, the question will be put to the audience and discussed.

During the discussion the chairman must keep his attention directed to the point at issue, and if any speaker wanders from the point or introduces personal or irrelevant matter, he must call him to order and to the subject before the meeting, which must not be lost sight of in a cloud of verbiage. The chairman will have to keep order, and, if there is much party feeling aroused, will use his influence to restrain excitement and keep unruliness in check.

At the end of the discussion, the votes or a show of hands will be taken in the usual manner. The chairman, unless a division is demanded, will decide whether the motion is lost or carried, and announce his decision to the meeting. If the number present is small the chairman may exercise his privilege of the casting vote; but this he will not do unless he considers the matter to be one of vital importance to any institution or constitution in which he takes a strong personal interest. In a matter of merely party interest he will do well to abstain from voting on an occasion when the voting shows that the opinion is about equally divided.

If an amendment has been moved to the original motion, it must be voted on first, for, if carried, it will replace the original motion and must itself be put to the vote a second time as a substantive motion: it will now be competent to move an amendment to it.

When the business for which the meeting was convened is terminated, the chairman will formally declare the proceedings to be at an end; but before he leaves the chair it is the custom for someone present to propose a vote of thanks to him for his conduct of the business. This will find a seconder, and being put to the meeting will, as a rule, be carried by acclamation without question.

The meeting may then be made "special," and various resolutions can be passed according to the terms upon which the Company or Society has been embodied. Another chairman may be elected, or the same man can officiate if requested to do so.

AT SOCIAL GATHERINGS

The chairman of a social gathering has a different office to perform. He takes his place before dinner and holds it to the end of the evening; though it happens occasionally that as President of a Company he may preside at the dinner and move someone else into the chair when the toasts come to be proposed.

The chairman will propose the toast of the Queen, and will call upon the proposers of and responders to other toasts, all these details having been settled beforehand; for it is not fair to let anyone be called upon for a toast or a response with no chance of arranging his line of thought or of *"studying his impromptus."*

It is usual at public dinners for a musical and elocutionary entertainment to be arranged, for which a programme will have been prepared. In the order of the programme the chairman will call for a toast, this to be followed by a song, recitation, or instrumental music; further, it will be the chairman's business, by tact, good-temper and management, to maintain the harmony of the evening and to discourage anything in the way of bad taste, and all this he should do in a spirit of good-fellowship.

The disposal of the guests with reference to the chairman or president is made according to precedence, the Royal Family having the lead, unless a certain personage is to be specially honoured, when he occupies the place on the right hand of the chairman, and the most important representative of Royalty present the place on the left hand. The guest of the evening is always seated at the right hand of the chair, the next in honour on the left, and so on according to rank and standing, distinguished guests being seated also near the top of the table, with notable members of the society or corporation in whose hall the dinner is given.

The toast of the Queen is usually given as soon as possible after the last course of the dinner is finished. Immediately after this toast the chairman will give out the notice "Gentlemen, you may smoke," or if ladies are present, "Ladies and gentlemen, you may smoke." There must be no smoking before the toast of the Queen is honoured, and for this reason the chairman should be on the *qui vive* to give "The Queen" as early as possible. In order that the waiters may clear the table, there is usually an interval of ten minutes between the permission to smoke and the announcement of the first item on the programme.

CHAPTER IX

DEBATING SOCIETIES

WHILE there is no royal road to proficiency in public speaking, practice is above all things essential, and for the beginner this is best acquired by joining a good debating club or society, and by frequently taking part in its discussions. He will thus get not only practice in the art of speaking, but much valuable information on a variety of topics; above all, he will in course of time overcome the nervousness that marks the novice and acquire the readiness of speech and quickness of thought that are, perhaps, the chief weapons in the public speaker's armoury.

And for a beginner, too, a debating club is perhaps more useful than a local Parliament; there is less formality, fewer rules and conventions have to be observed, and he is less likely to be overburdened by a feeling of the importance of the occasion or fear of criticism from his audience; moreover, there is more of "rough and tumble" debate, which is excellent in producing readiness and quickness.

When, however, the beginner feels quite at home in his own debating society, and feels, too, that his speeches carry weight there, he should seek a wider field and a different audience, for there is always a danger that, having grown accustomed to one audience and one kind of debate, he may fail to do himself justice elsewhere. It is then that local Parliaments are useful; and the speaker who has emerged successfully from the ordeal of both debating society and local Parliament need not fear to address almost any audience.

"CONSTITUTION" OF DEBATING SOCIETIES

But though, as has been pointed out, debating societies have rules less rigid and formal than those of local Parliaments, nevertheless, the rules should be sufficiently clear and precise to ensure the proper conduct of proceedings, and, while allowing for the interruption which enlivens, should check the disorder which reduces debate to chaos. A settled "constitution" and regular officers are therefore necessary.

Dealing with the latter first, the officers are generally: —

(1) President or Chairman.
(2) Vice-President (one or more).
(3) Treasurer.
(4) Secretary.
(5) Committee, which will include all the officers and five or seven elected members.

The PRESIDENT will, of course, take the chair at any meeting at which he is present, and will regulate the progress of debate and see that the rules are observed. His duties may be gathered from the chapter in this volume on the subject. In his absence the senior officer present, and in the absence of all officers, one of the Committee will take the chair.

The TREASURER, of course, has charge of the funds, and it is his duty to see that subscriptions are paid, and—a much more difficult task this—to endeavour to have a small balance on the right side at the end of the year. He is responsible for all payments, and should see that no money is expended except in the manner and for the objects provided by the rules.

The SECRETARY'S duties are manifold. He is in charge of all the Society's official correspondence, he keeps the Minute Book, or arranges with someone else to take Minutes of meetings at which he is not present, he arranges the details of joint debates with other societies, and is charged with the duty of seeing that members receive all official notices and announcements.

In most societies it is the duty of the COMMITTEE to decide all important matters arising within the society, and generally to manage its affairs and select suitable subjects for debate, as well as the leading speakers on each side for each meeting.

THE ART OF DEBATING

AN ORDINARY MEETING

After the customary reading and signing of Minutes, the election of new members, and the transaction of any other business that may have arisen, the Chairman will announce the motion or subject of discussion, and call upon the Opener, who will read a paper or make a twenty-minute speech from notes in accordance with local custom. Opinions differ upon the relative merits of these two courses. On the whole we incline to the written speech, otherwise the opening will be left exclusively to the more experienced. An utter collapse of the Opener—and a nervous youth speaking from notes often breaks down—means the spoiling of an evening.

The Opener, be he speaker or essayist, will probably be allowed fifteen or twenty minutes where ten minutes is the limit for ordinary speeches. Custom varies as to the procedure when he finishes. At most societies he is followed by an Opposer appointed beforehand, who is allowed the same time as the Opener; but some throw the discussion open to the meeting immediately, which we think distinctly preferable. Whether the formal reply is read or written it will have been prepared, and the Opposer will say what he has come there to say, whether it directly traverses the arguments of the Opener or not. Thus arguments are "knocked" that no one has set up and the arguments that *have* been adduced are ignored. In one of the famous controversies of the nineties Herbert Spencer wrote: "What I said has not been refuted by Mr. Frederic Harrison. What has been refuted I never alleged."

Taking an Opportunity.—Well, the opening is finished, and the formal opposing, if any, and now is the chance of our beginner. Let him jump up at the very first opportunity while his courage holds. It may not be the most suitable moment for the introduction of his particular line of argument, but it is the most suitable moment for *him*. His courage may never again be so high. Intending first speakers grow more and more nervous with waiting until they lose the ability to conquer their fears. Often they come away from a meeting after suffering agonies of stage-fright, to tear up in disgust the undelivered speech to which they have devoted so much pains. These devastating experiences may be repeated until the aspirant ceases to aspire and abandons his resolve to become a public speaker, to his own great loss and, perhaps, to that of others, for nervousness is often most conspicuous in the imaginative and artistic.

Overcoming Nervousness.—There is no panacea for speech-fright. The cure is gradual and effected by experience; therefore the beginner must see that he gets this experience without delay. It will help if he will solemnly resolve before the meeting that he will speak, however cogent the reasons may then seem for abstaining; for these reasons are thoughts "that quartered have but one part reason and every three parts coward." Having risen to his feet, let him stay up, however badly he may be faring. He will have his written speech in his pocket, and rather than sit down wholly discomfited let him read it remorselessly to the bitter end—a partial failure, of course. On the chance of his being driven to read, his exordium should not be along lines that reading would render ridiculous. We remember hearing a nervous youth read this: "Mr. Chairman, Ladies and Gentlemen—Although I have listened very carefully to the Opener, I have not been convinced by his arguments." To which the Opener, with cruelty quite uncalled for, replied, that as his critic must have written this before *hearing* the arguments, it was not strange that they had not convinced him.

It is by no means true that all beginners go through the agonies of nervousness and vacillation we have just described. Many escape them altogether. By some fortunate accident they get pushed into the waters of debate before they have had time to baulk themselves upon the brink, and being in and discovering that they can splash about as well as the others, they lose their water-shyness for good and all. Others, before resolution has had time to cool, or before they have formed resolutions, get cajoled into the water by an observant Chairman. There are times when the plunge seems less formidable, and the Chairman suggests the opportunity. A favourable season is after a speech of the business-experience type has been made. Most men feel that here is the kind of speech anyone can make. The facts are there waiting to be stated. A kindly Chairman will hold off the experienced speakers here, and give the boys a chance.

These "personal knowledge" speeches can be made by anyone, and are, therefore, useful at the start, but they lead nowhere, and should be discarded early by the ambitious learner, who after splashing around once or twice in these shallows should strike out boldly into the deeper waters of deduction, keeping his facile and fallible inductions as lifelines to which he may cling when in danger of sinking.

The ironical pushing home of a fairly obvious point—for irony is only safe in oratory when everyone can perceive that it is irony—is sometimes very effective, and the beginner should try a short speech on these lines when he sees an opening.

ORATORY VERSUS DEBATE

Oratory and debating are different arts, although they have much of their technique in common. Debating can be defined best by elimination. Every form of written or memorized speech is rejected *per se*. Nor is speaking at short notice to a resolution necessarily debating, although the two are often confounded. We once attended a debate upon *Capital Punishment*. Just as the meeting was starting it became known that the opposer wasn't coming. A man seated beside us who had considerable reputation as a speaker was pressed into the service, although he hadn't intended to speak. This is how he prepared himself for the ordeal. For perhaps three minutes he listened closely to the opener's speech, after which he gave himself to the preparation of his own. When his turn came he rose portentously.

SPEECH OPPOSING A MOTION ADVOCATING THE ABOLITION OF CAPITAL PUNISHMENT

Mr. Chairman, Ladies and Gentlemen,—

The mover of this resolution began by recalling an instance of miscarriage of justice. A brilliant young doctor was wrongly convicted of a foul murder and hanged. Twenty years afterwards a man confessed upon his death-bed that he was the murderer. Had the young doctor's sentence been life-long imprisonment instead of the barbarous irrevocable punishment of death, argued the opener, it would have been possible to right the wrong. I should like to be told how. Suppose his sentence had been imprisonment, and that after twenty years he had been released. Picture him as he stands blinking at the sun outside the prison gates; his poor hands calloused with degrading toil, hands once endowed with a surgeon's incredible skill; his eyes telling of an intellect "like sweet bells jangled, out of tune and harsh," and of a soul seared as by hot irons by twenty years of close intimacy with foul and brutal men. Well, there he stands. What are you going to do with him, Mr. Opener?

"Canst thou not minister to a mind diseased,
Pluck from the memory a rooted sorrow,
Raze out the written troubles of the brain?"

So far he had been debating. The rest of his speech, not being directed to anything that had been said, was not debating, but oratory at short notice. We can say, then, that a speech is a debating speech to the extent to which it is the result of listening. A hundred per cent. debater in the position of this man would have listened throughout to the opening, and so intently that his subsequent effort of speaking would have seemed a relaxation.

HOW A DEBATER LISTENS

If you have ever considered what it means to follow an able speaker, attacking his arguments *seriatim*, you will not need to be told that it implies the ability to think upon one's feet and to fashion sentences and arguments, introduction and peroration as one proceeds. How *can* one make any speech preparation while the opponent is speaking? *He* must have all the debater's attention, and a three-fold attention at that: what is being said must be taken in sentence by sentence; the argument must be weighed as a whole; and the argument itself must be considered in relation to the argumentation of which it forms a part. Further, each particular argument must not only be considered in relation to the argumentation, but it must also be compared with each other separate argument; for if it can be shown that the implications of one argument contradict those of another, the debater will score decisively. The discovery of such a discrepancy changes the whole plan of attack where speeches are strictly limited in time. The *seriatim* method might leave insufficient time to exploit the great discovery. The attack leads off with it prepared to follow the issue to its conclusion, and let, if need be, all else go. If he can make good here the battle is won.

CORNERING AN OPPONENT

Should the discrepancy be established there is no need for the attacker to try to wring an admission of error from his opponent. The audience have eyes. They can see when an issue is being dodged, and they know that it is tantamount to

5

retreat. Let the beaten foe withdraw from the field. Cornered he may strike back surprisingly. Frederick the Great lost the battle of Kunersdorf by not allowing a Russian Army to get away. There was more fight in these stubborn Russian peasants than he had supposed. But were cornering as safe as it is dangerous, it should have no place in friendly discussions. Win if you can, but why humiliate? When, however, upon a controversy hang great issues, amenities may go by the board. Abraham Lincoln, in a public discussion with Stephen Douglas, relentlessly wrung from him an admission favourable to Lincoln's own contention that America could not continue half slave-owning, half free, an admission fraught with tremendous consequences. No great National issues hang upon any debates our readers participate in; we therefore lay it down as a maxim—*avoid cornering*.

POUNCING

There is in the make-up of a truly great debater a touch of the eagle, ever ready to swoop down upon a worthy quarry, but leaving field mice and the like to the pouncings of lesser birds. The debater must ignore small game, as, for example, trifling errors in chronology. No gentleman would pillory grammatical *faux pas* or mispronunciations. In a district council debate this speech was made:—

"I suggest, Mr. Chairman, that we should act in accordance with the Latin adage: 'Suav-í-ter in modo. Fort-í-ter in re.'" Which elicited this:—

"The last speech was excellent in quality if somewhat open to criticism in the matter of quantity."

This of course is clever and the sting is hidden from the mispronouncer; but who can be sure that he may not have the taunt explained to him by some good-natured friend? No, let us keep on the safe side. Flouts and jeers and notable scorns are not permissible. Few of us can hope to become orators, but it is within our compass to prove ourselves men of good-will.

NON SEQUITURS

Non Sequiturs are of two kinds, those arising from confused thinking, and those occasioned by careless speech. A magistrate sentencing a prisoner said:—"You have been brought up in a Christian home, and have enjoyed the inestimable advantages of university and public school, instead of which you go about the country stealing ducks." Now this magistrate wasn't a fool. All unwittingly he has omitted a sentence that was in his mind, such as "By now you should be making headway in some honourable profession." Slips in debate of this nature should be ignored. It is a debater's business, however, to expose confusions of thought, which are the real *non sequiturs*, and fallacies of all kinds.

DESIRABLE WORDINESS

Critics of the art of writing often assume that the great desideratum is the expression of thought in the fewest words possible. (By this criterion Milton's sonnet upon his blindness must be adjudged of less literary value than a sixpenny telegram.) But an orator's aim is twofold: to express himself and to *impress* himself. This fewest words ideal is wholly inapplicable to oratory, which must be far more explicit and diffuse than writing, because missing a writer's meaning you can look back and capture it, whereas there is no *hearing back*. The spoken sentence uncaught is lost for ever. To prevent this, recourse is had to varied repetitions. The verbal texture of a good speech differs from that of a well-written essay. The speech has a larger proportion of nouns; elisions are minimized. Verbs and prepositions, far from being bundled out of sight, are brought into prominence. The writer's bane, the way a word already used insists upon suggesting itself as the only word, is the orator's blessing, bringing him many of his best effects, as witness this example: "It is to these unmanly forebodings; it is to these unworthy apprehensions; it is to the jealousies, misunderstandings and intolerances that we owe our wars." The unvaried repetition of the connecting little words gives a unity to the passage. These repetitions, valuable to the orator, are to the debater essentials. While his lips are uttering them his mind fashions the phrases they introduce.

THE ART OF REPLY

In Parliament the right of the opener of a debate to the last word is a privilege highly valued; but in debating and literary societies whose proceedings are limited to two hours' duration.

it is often waived. Perhaps the Chairman has conveyed a hint by allowing a member, who otherwise would have been shut out from the discussion, to encroach upon the time allotted to the opener's reply. A hurried answer to criticisms being in some respects worse than none, the opener may withdraw gracefully thus:—

"Mr. Chairman, Ladies and Gentlemen,—

"I can see some of you casting anxious glances at the clock. Fortunately it is not necessary for me to detain you. I have been denounced most eloquently, and defended with equal eloquence and better logic. I am quite content, therefore, to leave the decision to the meeting." Of course the opener can't ignore the discussion generally if it has been uniformly hostile.

Closing a discussion you are sure of applause if you balance conflicting criticisms thus: "Mr. A. found me too pessimistic, whereas it was my shallow, insincere optimism that disgusted Mr. B. Mr. C. had almost convinced me that my fiscal proposal, if carried out, would reduce grain prices to the ruin of farmers, when Mr. D. rose to demonstrate that these same deplorable measures would *raise* prices to the impoverishment of the consumer. The objections cancel themselves out like one of the cancellation sums of our boyhood—leaving nothing." This will send your own side into ecstasies, and generally will be regarded as a smashing reply and exceedingly brilliant. But it is a fallacy, notwithstanding. All objections are not of equal weight. Close economic reasoning that a certain proposed change would raise prices isn't to be balanced against the guess of an ignoramus that it would lower them. Each argument must be considered upon its own merits. A.'s logic must be met by logic; it cannot be overthrown in any other way. But this cancelling out reply is so popular, and, it may be added, so very easy to make, that it is almost useless to protest against it. Even Cabinet Ministers resort to it. "The member for —— has adduced statistics to prove that my estimates are excessive. Only yesterday the —— newspaper devoted a leader to showing that they are woefully deficient." The argument is that therefore the estimates in question must be correct. Utter rubbish!

If an easily attained seeming excellence in reply attracts you more than the prospect of learning by hard study and many failures to argue convincingly, this balancing of opposites argument will be your stand-by. But you might spare us the verbal absurdity. No cancellation sum can possibly show for its answer—**0**.

As a general rule the choice should be made between a fairly full reply or none at all. Your ox won't go into a teacup. But if a speaker has been notably long and tedious he can sometimes be annihilated by mere brevity.

CRUSHING BY CONTRAST

We give two illustrations.

A certain annual chapel meeting was marked by excessive and prolonged criticism. Through it all sat the chairman, his face as rigid as that of a Trafalgar Square lion. At last he rose. "Has any other brother or sister any suggestion to make for improving the ministrations of this chapel? No! Then let us thank God and sing hymn one hundred and three."

If the contrast between length and brevity can crush, so also can that between strength and levity. At the annual business meeting of a cricket and tennis club, a tennis devotee rose to complain that an undue proportion of the club's income was devoted to cricket. He spoke with uncalled-for asperity, and proved by elaborate statistics that, leaving out of count members whose allegiance was divided, there were in the club more tennis players pure and simple than cricketers. He was answered and annihilated thus from the chair:—

"Gentlemen,—

"It is a great satisfaction to me as president of this club to hear from Mr. —— that it contains ninety-seven tennis men who are pure and simple, and eighty cricketers who merit the same encomium."

Nothing more was ever heard of the protest. It had been laughed away.

SPECIMEN DEBATING SPEECHES

The following debating speeches:—

1. That Wireless is more Important than Aviation;
2. That Common Sense is more Essential than Genius to the Business Man;

3. That Sentiment is of Value in Business;
4. That Personality is an Acquirable Attribute—

will serve to show the reader on what lines debating speeches should be prepared and may be used as models upon which speeches on other subjects can be built up.

1. THAT WIRELESS IS MORE IMPORTANT THAN AVIATION

There is, I suppose, no achievement of which science may be more justly proud than the conquest of space. The world is a much smaller place to-day than it ever was, and nations are nearer to each other now than at any time since they were divided at the tower of Babel. The Story of Babel is a very true one, for might not mankind have built a tower reaching to the very heavens themselves had not the strife of tongues rent their forces and divided them into opposing and often hostile camps?

Division of tongues, leading, as it inevitably must do, to differences of manner and custom, forms a most effective barrier between nation and nation. Language is an intimate thing and penetrates those little idiosyncrasies which appear trivial, but are really the core of a people. I am sure my opponent to-night will not deny that the instrument which most effectively overcomes this subtle and intangible dividing line is, for that very reason, the most important discovery of our time.

In my opinion the greatest instrument for establishing true understanding between nations is the wireless. Flying touches only the externals; it takes a few people from one country and puts them down in another, and all that it has achieved in that operation is to exhibit samples of one nation to another. The visitors see only the externals; they cannot penetrate into the thoughts, the joys and sorrows, the traditions and aspirations of their host. But it is just this intimate touch which wireless gives us: we can listen to the everyday news—and, what is more important, the nature of what is called news—of a neighbouring state. We hear their music and the manner of its rendering, we listen to the educational labours of its teachers, the pronouncements of its statesmen, and most important of all, the amusement of its children. A knowledge of the language is not an essential to the formation of some conception of the customs and habits of our neighbours. The mere feeling of proximity alone does its beneficial work.

The conclusion that may be reached is that deep down beneath externals nations are marvellously similar in the real things of human life: if this is the impression, it is, surely, the surest safeguard against misunderstanding and hostility. It is an impression difficult to gain by short visits to foreign shores, especially in countries where the courtesy of the inhabitants often impels them to provide, as far as possible, the native conditions of their guests. No one could know France through a stay, however protracted, in Paris, for he finds there either a reproduction of his home conditions, or else certain of the least admirable of the French characteristics exaggerated out of all recognition. But a man who from his suburban villa constantly listens in to the programmes designed for the entertainment of the French family circle, might come somewhere near a very real appreciation of French genius.

In these democratic days the inventions of science stand at the bar of the people and are judged by their capacity for adaptation by the masses. We must admit, I think, that flying at present, and even as far as can be ascertained for long years to come, must redound chiefly to the advantage of the rich. The cost of flying exceeds the first-class railway fare, and even with the development of huge planes the numbers carried must be very limited. The merchandise carried by air must be costly, and is very largely confined to articles expensive because of their rarity and fragility. That hundreds or even thousands have an easy and speedy means of travel must be an insignificant feature in the life of a nation composing many millions. There must also be many lonely places of the earth where the aeroplane can never penetrate owing to their inaccessibility. Broadcasting, however, from its inception has been democratic. Even good receiving sets are not expensive, and there are apparatuses graded to suit all pockets. A dweller in the depressing streets of a London suburb can hear the nightingale singing in a country garden, while the lonely farmer in the wilds of Canada can be kept in touch with the activities of great cities.

I have endeavoured to describe the invention of wireless broadcasting as one of the most potent forces working for the moral uplift of mankind and the future peace of the world. Aviation, whatever may be said in its favour, can be turned into the most deadly weapon of human destruction. It is by the flying machine alone that belligerents are enabled to invade the peaceful areas of their opponents, attacking the centres of peaceful cities and scattering death and terror among helpless women and innocent children. The aeroplane removes the horrors of battle from the armies of fighting men and transplants them amongst those who are least able to defend themselves. Such a development is a heavy price to pay for the benefits that can otherwise be reaped.

So far I have dealt with these two inventions from an international standpoint, and many of my remarks have been prophecies of the future rather than records of accomplished facts. Broadcasting, although its province is bound to extend very rapidly, is at present much nearer its infancy than is aviation. The average listener is still for the most part limited to the activities of his own local station.

Even so, however, broadcasting is wielding an influence in the homes of England, be they palaces or cottages, which is far beyond the powers of aviation. The voice of the most learned scientists, the most competent critics, and the most popular musicians brings culture and learning to many who would never have gained it in the rough discipline of the schoolroom. There are, of course, faddists who deplore that the ear of the nation is becoming corrupt by the failure to obtain perfect reception, and undoubtedly many worthy people have suffered financially from the effects of broadcasting. In spite of this, can it be denied that a higher standard of taste and judgment is being set up, almost subconsciously, in the minds of our people? Such faults as exist are certain to be eradicated in time, and the companion invention of television, developed, will do much to remedy some of the more obvious disadvantages under which we labour to-day.

It is a commonplace that in the last century scientific achievement outgrew the moral advance of Europe, and that while our standards of comfort and efficiency increased, the advantages that should have accrued therefrom were limited by failure to attain a corresponding moral progress. Commercial competition became keen to the verge of brutality, and wars more ruthless and frequent. In wireless we may find a means not only of increasing our material prosperity, but also of making human nature more as its Creator intended it to be.

I submit that wireless is of greater benefit than aviation to the human race.

2. THAT COMMON SENSE IS MORE ESSENTIAL THAN GENIUS TO THE BUSINESS MAN

This is an age of specialization, and to attain success in modern life a man must choose his mark and aim straight for it. I am one who has chosen commerce and am not ashamed to call myself a plain business man. As such I should like to consider what is the best equipment for those who desire to follow the path that for so many years I have had to tread. Much has of late been written about the "secret of success," but, in my judgment, the whole matter boils down to two very simple words—"common sense."

Do not think for one moment that I disparage what we call "genius"; it is surely to the great intellects of the world that we owe the great discoveries of science which have circled the world with the rings of our commerce. It is again to genius that we are indebted for the sweet music of the singer, the noble vision of the artist, and in fact all those ennobling qualities that have raised mankind above the beast. My point to-night is simply this—that great intellect is not essential or even helpful to the business man, as such.

Now let me define my terms: it is quite true, no doubt, that common sense is only a certain application of brain power; may we define common sense as the average amount of reasoning power possessed by ordinary everyday people? When we speak of a man as possessing "genius" we usually imply, not that others have no brains, but that he has something above the usual amount of grey matter possessed by the man in the street. It is something that marks him out and distinguishes him from the common herd, and therefore tends to hold him rather aloof from his fellows. The same thing occurs wherever a man is unable to place himself within the very small limit of variation from type allowed by mankind. The giants of old lived, we are told, in caves, while Diogenes sought the seclusion of his lonely tub. Now this is fatal in business. The merchant must be a man of the world with the rumours of the market, the bustle of the docks in his ears. He awaits, with his wares to sell, the stranger is there with gold in his hand—he must bestir himself and meet him. It follows, therefore, that in so far as it is necessary for a business man to be easy of approach, ready to be all things to all men, brains tend to be a disadvantage rather than an asset.

My second point is that the man of brains tends to be a specialist. It must, I think, necessarily be so, for few men, however great their genius, can take, like Sir Francis Bacon, all knowledge for their province. The great mind must work from certain data, just as the carpenter must select his necessary tools: these data will be scientific, mathematical, or literary according to his individual bent. The learned man seldom has aptitude for all these subjects. The mathematician reads the "Paradise Lost" and wonders what it proves, while the poet ignores his Euclid as pettifogging jargon. Such concentration upon one subject breeds abstraction, and the events of everyday life rush by unheeded and unknown.

Not thus is made the business man: more suitable to him is that little knowledge of a host of things, which may be dangerous, but which is, like many dangerous things, extremely useful. He needs his figures in his counting-house; he has to solve his little legal problems; he must have some knowledge of railways and shipping, and some understanding of markets and exchanges: above all he must be a psychologist studying continually the aspirations and ambitions of his competitors and of his subordinates. Abstractions he must avoid; he must be quick to note the experience of others and for ever ready to turn the fortuitous happenings of chance to his own advantage.

I expect my friend who is opposing me to-night will tell you I have dwelt upon too low a scale. He will, no doubt, contend that the modern business man requires vision; it is essential, he will say, that the business man should look ahead and be prepared in advance to meet the demands of the future, and at the same time he must be a deep scholar of the manners and customs of his own contemporaries, with a view to increasing their demand for his goods, and to adjusting his supplies to meet modern requirements. No one would deny the truth contained in this statement, but it is not the true function of the business man to carry it out. Men of genius are necessary in commerce; the inventor, the scientist, the expert and specialist, are all necessary in business, but they are not business men. They are servants hired at wages, and not men venturing their own or other people's money for profit. It is not the function of the business man to discover improvements rendering his commodities more useful to the nation; it is, however, his duty to take care that these improvements are made and carried out by people able to do it, and that the results of their work are of service to his ends.

The business man is the driving force, inspiring it may be the whole body with his own vitality and activity; but behind him there must be the specialist who is the nerve system of the whole organism. It may be that no really big business man has time to give his wares just that distinction which shall make them excel those of his rival, but there must be someone whose function it is to do so. It takes a clever man to choose his specialists aright, and to make sure that their labours, obscure though their details may be to him, produce the right result in the long run. In other words, he must be a man of supreme common sense.

Thus I think it follows from what I have said that common sense is more necessary than genius in business.

3. THAT SENTIMENT IS OF VALUE IN BUSINESS

To-night I want to ask this House to agree with me that sentiment is of value in business. It is a proposition that would have sounded strange in the ears of our forbears. To them business was business; and nothing was allowed to interfere with what they regarded as the stern economic law of supply and demand. They were encouraged in this view by the then infant science of political economy which insisted on regarding human beings as machines without souls, necessary as other machinery to the production of wealth. Further the State was dominated by the theory of *laissez faire* under which the stern laws of economics were to be pushed to their logical conclusion. It may well be that in our day we have gone to the other extreme, and many politicians give such importance to what may be termed sentimental considerations, as virtually to exclude sound commercial principles entirely. As a reaction against this prevailing tendency in modern politics, many business men are still inclined to discount the value of sentiment as a factor in business success.

No one would deny, of course, that it is possible to have too much even of a good thing, but in spite of this I am here to contend to-night that sentimental considerations have their place, and a very large place, in modern business.

In business the employer is dealing with men and not

machines, and men in all ages have responded more readily to the human touch than to the demands of the most perfectly organized routine. In military organizations this has always been recognized, and the greatest generals are those who in days of hardship and peril have been ready to waive the privileges of their rank and share with their men the heat and burden of the battlefield. A little recognition of long and faithful service, an occasional confession that they too are touched by human frailties, are the most potent means an employer has of gaining the affection of his subordinates.

How happy are the closing days of an employer who knows that he has travelled along the road of life from youth to old age with many of his employees and that the bright as well as the dark days have not been entirely unknown to any of them but through good or ill they have stood together in their determination to do their bit by the old firm. Sheer sentiment! My friend may say so, but would business be the worse for it to-day? In these days of combinations and amalgamations, however, it is clearly impossible in most cases for employers to establish such personal relations with every member of their staff. It may indeed only be possible to try to vitalize or impersonify the firm or company as an ideal, and to endeavour to inspire its servants with something of that feeling which the average boy has for his school. If employees can be made to believe that their business house is the best and most efficient organization of its kind, they will not be long in turning this ideal into an actual fact. Where athletics can be encouraged and provided for, the friendly rivalry of the sports field has been found to make commercial competition the healthier. The establishment of recreation clubs has also a great sentimental value as they provide a pivot around which the affections of the men for the firm can centre: but club premises of this kind must not be dingy and dirty but worthy of the high ideals of the organizations identified with them.

I do not blush to place proposals of this kind before you, when I find them all advocated and adopted by such a great industrialist as the late ——. In the centre of his model village there is not only a noble church but also a spacious hall upon the lofty walls of which are hung the portraits of every employee of long standing and good record. Far wider, however, than the material interest of any one organization is the value of sentiment to commerce in general. In the Middle

Ages every trade and calling had its own Guild regulating its own terms of admission, standard of efficiency, and making provision for the care of its members in sickness and distress. Membership of such a Guild bestowed the right to a distinctive dress and badges denoting the skilled craftsman and the apprentice. There was no priority between the different Guilds, and membership of any one of them betokened the highest distinction to which a man could attain.

In this modern unsentimental age, we are accustomed to think and speak of some callings as low and mean and fail to recognize that all honest labour is worthy of equal dignity and honour. If a man thinks his daily labour is mean and unworthy, he will become mean and unworthy himself. If one kind of avocation is believed to be more respectable than another, the normal distribution of labour will be hampered and the work of the nation impeded. Would it not be well that every service should be revitalized by the appreciation of noble traditions of a worthy past and high ideals for a glorious future? This is sentiment in business—I submit we want it!

4. THAT PERSONALITY IS AN ACQUIRABLE ATTRIBUTE

If one were asked to quote the best-known line of Shakespeare it would probably be "Some men are born great, some achieve greatness, and some have greatness thrust upon them." To-night I have to ask you to endorse the statement of the immortal bard that "some achieve greatness."

First and foremost let me state that by greatness I do not mean wealth nor even what some call "success in life." These are too often the result of mere chance, the luck of life's gamble, and indeed far from revealing greatness they frequently merely reveal to man his contemptible littleness. Greatness is a much more elusive quality: John Bunyan in his prison house, Sam Johnson in his dusty lodging, Napoleon Bonaparte on his Imperial Throne were indisputably "great," and would have been great in rags or in ermine. Greatness is not to be confused with goodness: Satan of the "Paradise Lost" is, as has often been said, a gentleman and a great gentleman, but he was not intended by Milton to be good. Sainthood, however, may sometimes be an indication of greatness as it was in St. Francis, and greatness may even become confused with sainthood as in the case of St. Joan of Arc. The fact is, greatness must have an outlet, and that outlet may be either good or bad: and there remains sufficient virtue in humanity to perpetuate the memory of good great men rather than bad.

It follows, I think, from what I have said that greatness is an illusive quality inherent in an individual and may perhaps approximate to a particular kind of personality.

Now I am willing to admit that the numbers of those who are born great and of those who have greatness thrust upon them must be far in excess of those who achieve greatness: and I shall even agree with my friend who opposes this evening if he contends, as I have no doubt he will, that many have achieved greatness merely because they are born great.

Yet I contend it is still possible for one who has no particular gifts at birth, to achieve by his own volition a distinct personality which in contrast with other personalities may be called great. The personality which is achieved rather than innate is usually obtained by means of some external agency, and I think I can best illustrate my contention by referring briefly to a few of the many agencies that have produced greatness. One of the most common is the vision of a high ideal. This is not the place in which religion may be discussed, but no doubt instances occur in all religions, disguised though they may be under various names, of the human soul being suddenly enlarged by the vision of the Infinite. The inspiration may be national or political, especially among oppressed people and in hard times. Garibaldi seems to have been an ordinary enough person in his youth until fired by the vision of a free and United Italy, when he gradually achieved a personality worthy of a national hero.

Secondly, greatness of personality may be achieved by perseverance, and indeed from the dictum that genius is two per cent. inspiration and ninety-eight per cent. perspiration it may well be argued that perseverance is a necessary ingredient of personality. The great actor or judge who has left the impress of his personality upon his profession for all time, has first by unremitting toil and severe self-discipline acquired a complete knowledge of his craft. The human mind shrinks from the weary drudgery of concentration, and is ever seeking to regale itself with scraps and pickings from the surface of things. Hence most men subconsciously follow the line of least resistance, or are content so long as they are no worse or no better than their neighbours. It is by the discipline of mind necessary to perseverance that personality is found in one man distinguishable from that of his fellows.

Thirdly, greatness of personality may be possessed by the failures of the world, by the people who are born out of their age. It is most commonly found among those whose lot it is to suffer or to sorrow. Personality comes of that greatness of spirit which refuses to yield but holds valiantly on against myriad foes; which refuses to become crabbed or embittered by adversity, but rises triumphant over every disaster.

Whether personality can be acquired without the operation of any external agency has not to be decided. No man is free entirely from the influence of his environment, or from the reflections of everyday events upon his innermost being. Any man who has become master of his own soul and is at peace within himself has achieved personality and greatness.

IMPROMPTU SPEECHES

But we visualize a reader who is determined to achieve success by another route. Not for him the written and memorized speech. He has a little experience at proposing votes of thanks to the secretary of the house benefit society, etc., and he knows that he can express his thoughts clearly and forcibly for two or three minutes, without any preparation. He argues that there is no difference in principle between a two-minute speech and a ten. He is quite right. Ten minutes upon a subject you understand is no time at all. A disputant in a railway carriage, if his remarks are not interrupted, will often argue without a break for longer than that, and never once be gravelled for lack of a word. The only thing that prevents us all from speaking upon our feet as freely is lack of confidence. The mere fact that our young friend is attracted towards the extempore method suggests that he has plenty of nerve.

But he must prepare his speech so far as mastering the subject, and he would be well advised to jot down a number of points, but without feeling that he has to speak upon them all. They are useful in the event of his being brought suddenly to a full stop by finding himself in an argumentative cul-de-sac. If he really has confidence upon his feet he will talk much longer upon each point than he had anticipated, so let the most important of the points be written in red ink. Suppose he gets off to a good start, don't let him give a thought to anything but the argument in hand (when that fails he can look at his notes). Let him drive it home with illustrations, statistics, and pleading, for the craving to convince often removes nervousness; and let him not switch off abruptly from a topic that is going well to another suggested by his notes, upon which he may be floored.

The impromptu-speech evening is invaluable for gaining recruits to the ranks of the society's speakers. The routine varies —a very common plan being to have only one subject, upon which members speak in order determined by lot, being excluded from the hall until their respective turns to speak arrive. We give an example of an impromptu speech delivered under these conditions. The speaker is almost the last to come on. He doesn't know what has been already said, but believes that all have spoken in favour of the project (of which every sensible person must approve) and that affirmative arguments have been repeated *ad nauseam*. Therefore he takes the opposite side, being careful, however, to show by exaggeration that he is talking nonsense.

IMPROMPTU SPEECH AGAINST ACQUIRING AN OPEN SPACE FOR THE PEOPLE

Mr. Chairman, Ladies and Gentlemen,—

I can imagine the arguments that have been used by the speakers who have preceded me—all of them favouring the affirmative. Every one has begun by saying that open spaces like this are the lungs of our city. Your laughter shows me that I have guessed aright. Lungs! Why, their own stupid metaphor confounds them. A man needs two lungs only—our suburb already is blessed with two spacious commons. Do we want more? Would a man be improved if you gave him an indefinite number of lungs—crowding his trunk with lungs to the exclusion of other organs?

We are warned that unless we raise a certain sum of money houses will be built on ——. Mere houses—homes for young couples! Isn't it dreadful? Mere homes!

You, Mr. Chairman, have been heard to boast that in boyhood you used to shoot snipe on the site of the Seven Sisters

Road. Suppose in those days some millionaire had bought up all the land for miles north of Holloway Station, that stood there in those days, and presented it to the public to be kept for ever as an open space. Would this have been a boon to London or a curse? Can we hesitate about our answer? Not even to preserve your snipe-shooting, Mr. Chairman, would we give up our Seven Sisters Road. Through the beauty spot which some of you would so wantonly preserve, there may (if this atrocious proposal is rejected) in the lifetime of some of my hearers run a thoroughfare as soul-satisfying as the Seven Sisters Road—as uplifting as Upper Street, Islington, itself. For these reasons I spurn indignantly the proposal of acquiring —— as an open space for the people.

FOR THIS OCCASION ONLY

"Speech Makers" are addressed, usually, exclusively to people who want to make speeches, ignoring the large class who *don't* want to make speeches, but on some particular occasion are impelled to by obvious self-interest, burning religious conviction, or concern for the welfare of some club or society. We will consider in turn a slave of each of these urges.

Self-interest will make a shareholder, who is gravely dissatisfied with the way his company is being run, resolve to raise a protest at the forthcoming annual business meeting. Our first word of advice is, prepare your protest, write it out *in extenso*, learn it, rehearse it. This would seem too obvious to be worth stating did one not know that the inexperienced are amazingly trustful of the inspiration of the moment. Having learnt *how* to make his protest, our friend must ascertain *when* to make it; for a Chairman won't allow the proceedings to be interrupted except at certain stages. He cannot. Failing other means of obtaining information, recourse must be had to the secretary before the meeting begins. While our friend with his notes in his hand, his written speech in his breast pocket, and a sinking feeling at the pit of his stomach sits waiting for the auspicious moment we would whisper this final counsel:—"When you rise, complete the operation before looking towards the chair. We have seen interrupters meet the Chairman's eye when they were in the course of rising, and under its medusa glare they have remained as if turned to stone throughout their futile and feeble remarks, half up, half down, in a position that was neither standing nor sitting, but what the children call 'crookeying.'

"When firmly on your feet turn to the chair and obtain tacit or explicit leave to make your protest. Then immediately look away. It will not help the flow of your remarks to watch the Chairman writing on a slip of paper 'Who is this fellow?' to see the folded note travelling to the Secretary and observe his reply in shoulder shrug that you are one of the ephemera and must be allowed your momentary buzz and flutter before passing out of existence. Keep your eyes off everyone and your thoughts away from yourself (think of next year's dividend which may be passed unless you succeed in shaking up these old duffers) and all will go well."

Or the scene of a first and last appearance may be the Annual Assembly of a great religious denomination. To address such an audience, half of whom are themselves professional orators, is an ordeal indeed, and nothing but a burning conviction that he has a message would nerve a novice to undergo it. But he has this burning conviction. Perhaps he knows that the leaders are working towards union with another denomination, which he thinks would be disastrous. If no one else denounces it he will, he *must*. We will suppose that having been well coached he rises at the right moment, and has been invited by the chairman to make his objection from the platform. He must jump at this, although it certainly does seem more formidable than speaking from the floor. He will find it much less so. Speakers who have graduated from small debating societies are surprised when they make their debut as platform speakers to find how easy it is. Similarly with singers. Perhaps why one feels less nervous speaking from a platform is because it sinks the audience below you. You can forget them.

Before this much daring novice starts upon the last stage of his perilous adventure, we would say to him, "Walk deliberately. Don't hurry your steps up the aisle. Go over your opening sentences in your mind. This pause is whetting the curiosity of the audience: they are being prepared for you. And as you value your cause, don't open your lips until you are installed on the platform and facing four-square the great throng whom you hope to influence. A common effect of nervousness is to make men in your position begin to speak as they walk up the aisle. The effect to those behind the walking orator or orating walker, is that words seem to be streaming out through his ears. It always causes laughter and wastes, worse than wastes, the exordium."

Our enthusiast, having escaped these pitfalls, begins his speech with a fair chance of succeeding. If he entirely forgets himself in his message he may be, for just this one occasion, an impressive speaker. In all arts the mystery is the way sincerity enters into and ennobles every detail of execution in public speaking, informing tone, gesture and elocution.

It is a big drop from a great assembly where a man contends for things of the spirit, to a cricket club, and a non-speaker rising to oppose the Chairman's suggestion to re-elect the old committee *en bloc*, but there is the same sincerity. Fresh blood is needed or the club will decline. The situation occurs very often: the speech delivered we report verbatim as likely to help many.

SPEECH AGAINST ELECTING EN BLOC THE OLD
COMMITTEE OF A CRICKET CLUB

Mr. Chairman, Gentlemen,

I wish to oppose this suggestion that has come to us from the chair that we should re-elect *en bloc* our old committee, because I think the old committee is *too* old, and it is time we brought in younger men. I wish to bring others to my way of thinking, which must be my excuse for making a frontal attack upon the suggestion, instead of turning its flank by putting up a new name or new names. They are splendid fellows, these old Committee Men, but they have ceased to be splendid cricketers. They were both when they came on the Committee, and were elected originally because they *were* both. I want to see elected to-night just such a committee as these old friends of ours formed ten years ago. Our rules contemplate a Committee that includes a fair proportion of match players. To-day not one of the Committee is in the team except when, in the absence of the Captain, he takes command of it, to carry out our rules. How absurd! We play a man who is out of practice—a good man who has lapsed into golf, perhaps, play him for his captaincy alone, when he is the worst of all captains, because, rarely coming down to the nets, he knows little about the respective capabilities of his men. We must introduce new blood, Mr. Chairman, if our Club is to continue.

This shouldn't give offence. Silence is not golden when truth is so much less injurious than horrible imaginings.

SELF-IMPROVEMENT

Having made the first plunge—whether by impromptu speech, business-experience contribution, or more ambitiously by an argument from first principles, does not matter—let our novice press himself upon the Secretary as an opener of discussions, and this without any scruples about his incompetency for such high matters or pity for future audiences. If they can't listen indulgently to public speakers in the making, let them stay away. A debating society is no place for them. This opening may prove less of an ordeal than the first short speech. The announced Opener *knows* that he must speak, and *when*. It is uncertainty that sickens. Let him also make full use of all the auxiliary aids that his society supplies, reciting at all elocutionary meetings, reading essays on the essay nights, and whenever criticisms are invited being quick to oblige with one. He must never miss an impromptu-speech competition, or a business meeting, at the latter being quick to second adoption of report and accounts, to propose Committee men, and to invite the Secretary to express himself more lucidly.

RULES OF A DEBATING SOCIETY

Each Society will, of course, make its own rules, and these will vary according to circumstances.

The rules generally will come under eight heads.

1.—THE CLUB.—Rules under this head will fix the name of the club, its object, its place and time of meeting.

2.—MEMBERSHIP.—Under this rules will be provided for the nomination and election of members, entrance fee and subscription, and penalty for non-payment, which is generally suspension after notice, followed if necessary by expulsion.

3.—OFFICERS.—The number and names of Officers will be fixed, their term of office, the method of proposal and election, and their duties when elected.

4.—MEETINGS.—These rules fix the times and days of meetings, providing for a regular or ordinary meeting and for special meetings to be called by the Secretary, on a requisition from a certain number of members, or by the Committee. They will also lay down what business must be transacted at a special meeting—e.g., alteration of rules.

5.—CONDUCT OF MEETINGS.—Here will be described the ordinary procedure. The number of members to make a quorum, the Chairman's duties, his powers, and the order of business at a meeting will be defined. Rules will also be laid down to regulate debate, allotting time for opening speeches and ordinary speeches and reply, and for taking the vote.

6.—SELECTION OF SUBJECTS.—This is generally allotted by the rules to the Committee, though often it is ordered that the Secretary shall keep a suggestion book.

7.—RULES AND ALTERATION.—This section provides for the making of new rules and altering old ones, and contains regulations as to giving notice of proposed changes in the Society's constitution, and making such changes, and for the enforcement of the rules.

8.—MISCELLANEOUS.—Under this head the rules will deal with such subjects as the keeping of attendance books, the duty of members to attend meetings, the admission of visitors, etc.

In conclusion, it should be said that, however informal the proceedings, speakers should be very careful always to get up the subject of debate before the meeting, otherwise they can hope to derive little benefit from it, and, having no fixed scheme in their minds, will be apt to fall into bad habits, such as hesitancy and prolixity.

CHAPTER X

LOCAL PARLIAMENTS

THERE are in the United Kingdom at the present time a number of Debating Societies calling themselves "Parliaments," which have been organized to give members the opportunity of ventilating political and social questions on the basis of Parliamentary procedure.

These Parliaments have in many instances been very successful in developing debating talent, and in discovering the party preponderance in certain districts, and therefore in indicating the feeling of the country upon important questions of the day.

It has appeared to the publishers that a brief *résumé* of the chief points to be observed in the formation and conduct of such Parliamentary Debating Societies may be usefully included in the present volume; and they have accordingly had the following rules compiled, principally from actual "Parliamentary Procedure" as set forth by Lord Farnborough, who, as Sir Erskine May, had been the Clerk of the House of Commons.

The Rules and Regulations have been revised and, when necessary, adapted to local parliamentary necessities by an experienced hand. The assistance here given will, the publishers believe, be found useful to anyone engaged in mimic legislative debates.

The following Rules or "Standing Orders" are based upon experience :—

It will be necessary to have a book in which every member must enter his name and address when he pays his subscription for the year, or for the session, as may be decided by the Council. To each member is usually allotted a constituency which he retains either for a year or during his membership of the club.

The OFFICERS of a Parliamentary Debating Society should be as follows, and must be members of the society.

(1) The Speaker.
(2) Chairman of Committees (or Deputy-Speaker).
(3) Clerk of the House.
(4) Deputy-Clerk and Secretary.
(5) Treasurer.

The COUNCIL should consist of seven or nine members, the officers of the House being *ex officio* members of it. The Council may advisedly be selected from different political parties, as evenly balanced as possible. The Council should be elected on the first night of the session, and continue in office until the first night of the ensuing session. A fresh election of Council and Officers will then take place.

The President of the Council is elected by the Council, who in a body have the control of the funds through the treasurer, and the inspection of the accounts, etc., rendered by him. A vacancy in the Council may be filled up by that body at the first meeting after the announcement of such vacancy to the House in session. Five out of nine members form a quorum, and so on in proportion.

Notices of a Council meeting should be sent out by the Secretary at least one week before the date named for the meeting. (For this and other reasons it is advisable that the Secretary should be a paid official and responsible to the Council.)

The MEETINGS of a Local Parliament may be called weekly, at an hour most convenient to the majority of the members. This time should be fixed upon at a preliminary general meeting of the members, who can at the same time elect the officers, etc., of the Parliament. The regulations proposed should be submitted to this preliminary meeting and formulated after full discussion.

The subscriptions being paid, and the members elected being present at the specified time, the first proceeding will consist in *reading the Minutes of the previous meeting*. This must always be done first after the Speaker has taken the chair; or, if considered desirable, the Speaker may put the question to the House that "the Minutes be taken as read." This will save time.

After the reading of the Minutes of the previous meeting will follow the introduction to the Speaker of newly elected members, and the names of newly proposed members will be recorded.

The newly elected members should be accompanied by their respective proposers and seconders, and should advance up the floor of the House to the Speaker's chair, and be formally introduced to him by name, and as the Members for the Constituencies they have severally elected to represent.

When all the new members have been introduced, then those whose names have been submitted, with their addresses, and the names of their proposers and seconders, are read to the House, and they will be elected by the Council at the following Council meeting if no objection is lodged, and may be introduced as new members at the following meeting of the Parliament.

When any member presents himself at the table to pay his subscription, the Clerk or Secretary shall request him to enter his name and address and Constituency in the Members' Book, and the Secretary or Clerk shall enter his name in the "Constituency" Book; and if the place has a member already allotted to it, the member must choose another place to represent.

Members take their places to the right or left of the Speaker, according as their party is in or out of office. The front seats on the right are occupied by the Ministry, those on the left by the Leaders of the Opposition.

After the introduction of, and the proposals for, new members have been completed, Notices of Questions and of Motions should be handed in, and either read by the members who wish to bring them forward, or handed in *in duplicate* to the Clerk of the House at the table. He will then read them, and the Secretary will see that the Ministry have the questions to answer by next meeting. The motions will then be proceeded with in the same way, and when those of which previous notice had been given have been answered or debated, the adjourned debate (if any) will be resumed.

The above is the procedure which will be found perfectly suitable to Local Parliaments and in accordance with usage. It is desirable that all routine business should be conducted as expeditiously as possible, as the members generally will be interested only in the debate. No member is allowed to speak on a subject more than once during each debate.

RULES AND REGULATIONS FOR
LOCAL PARLIAMENTARY DEBATING SOCIETIES

The SPEAKER is the controller of the House: all debate ceases when he rises, and his dictum must be accepted as final. He has a casting vote when parties are equal, and may give it either way; but experience teaches that he gives it to the "Noes." His duty is to keep the debate in the proper channel and to enforce the rules of the House. It is customary to bow to the Speaker when entering or leaving the House, and no member or stranger wearing his hat must sit in the House in presence of the Speaker.

Members must not pass and repass between the Speaker and the member addressing the House.

No stranger must seat himself or be permitted to remain in any portion of the House set apart for members only.

When a member is in possession of the House all the rest should be silent, or at any rate no audible interruption should be made; and no periodical should be read unless for information to be used in connection with the debate.

Speaking.—In speaking in the House a member must look to the Speaker and address him, and keep strictly to the point of discussion. He must not allude to previous debates that session unless he wish to move that a question be reopened, or a decision be rescinded. He must then conclude with a Motion to that effect.

When a Motion has been made and then seconded, after due notice has been given of the member's intention to propose any question for consideration, it is then put to the House by the Speaker; but if the Motion be not seconded it is dropped.

A Motion, if unopposed, may be made without previous notice; but if subsequently anyone objects to it the proposer must withdraw it.

In the absence of the Speaker the chair will be taken by his Deputy; but if it should happen that the Deputy-Speaker also is absent, then the House must elect one of its members to the position. The nomination may be challenged, and a show of hands will decide the point, and so on till a selection be approved.

The RULES for DIVISIONS are those generally in force in the House of Commons, the Tellers being appointed by the Speaker; and these gentlemen in pairs receive the votes as the members file in to the right or left lobby, according as they are "Ayes" or "Noes." The Tellers then respectively hand the papers to the Speaker, who reads the numbers, and declares which party has the advantage, in the usual way.

We can only thus indicate a few of the leading points to be observed in the formation and arrangement of a Parliamentary Debating Society. Every such society must be influenced more or less by local conditions, which will change; but the chief points to be observed are touched upon above—the details can easily be filled in from any work upon Parliamentary Procedure.

FORMATION OF A MINISTRY

The "Ministry" should be formed by the elected Leader of the strongest political party, provided their means and opportunities are sufficient to do so. The Government should at first, if possible, be of the same politics as the actual Government of the country. But they may be compelled to resign by the rejection of a Bill, or a Vote of Censure, etc., being carried against them.

The Leader of the Ministerial Party will choose his colleagues, and will nominate them to various posts corresponding, when practicable, to those actually in the Cabinet. These "Ministers" must carefully study the duties and the difficulties encountered by the various departments they represent. He must find subjects for debate, compose the "Queen's Speech," and introduce Bills and other matter for discussion—in correspondence with the Leader of the Opposition. The subjects put up for debate are generally those at the moment before the House at Westminster.

When the Ministry resigns (or is defeated) the Leader of the Opposition will take office if prepared to do so; or he may permit the hitherto existing Ministry to resume the business and carry on the government until the end of the session, if his party is not sufficiently strong to conduct it. In many Local Parliaments the whole Ministry, save the Prime Minister, is usually changed each year. Fresh talent is then introduced and all members are given a chance to hold higher and more responsible posts.

A SUMMARY OF POINTS VITAL TO THE SPEAKER

There are certain points that the would-be speaker must remember, for if he does not keep them in mind he can never hope to become an efficient and forceful speaker.

He must remember that—

(1) He should think clearly and decide exactly what he wants to say. If he is muddle-headed he cannot hope to speak clearly.

(2) He must decide what to say and what not to say; that is, he must suit his speech, as far as length goes, to the time available. He should deal with one subject clearly and adequately rather than gloss over several aspects in a perfunctory manner.

(3) He must arrange a good preoration, or commencement, and must *make certain* of a telling ending or peroration. If a speaker knows where, when and how to end, he at least has a straw to clutch at if the worst happens and he forgets his points and comes to a dead end—he can finish.

(4) He should get up on the platform, if possible, and should not commence speaking until he is standing erect and facing his audience squarely.

(5) He must pitch his voice so that those at the back of the hall can hear; then all can hear. He should pick out one person from the audience and should endeavour to convince him; if he is won over the chances are that the rest of the audience will be with the speaker.

(6) He must not hurry, but must speak slowly, deliberately and very distinctly, and should pronounce every syllable in each word.

(7) He should use a natural tone if possible, and should pitch the voice a little low rather than too high.

(8) He must use his notes as little as possible, but if the notes alone are not sufficient to keep him under way, he must read his speech and read it through to the bitter end. He must do it openly, and should not try to hide the fact that his speech is being read.

(9) He should occasionally turn his head and shoulders from side to side, so as to address the audience on either side. He must not move his feet.

(10) Above all, he must be sincere and earnest.

PART II
SPECIMEN SPEECHES AND TOASTS

CHAPTER XI

LOYAL AND PATRIOTIC TOASTS

Note:—See *The Chief Toasts*, page 52.

1. LOYAL TOASTS

Proposed by the Chairman

LOYAL toasts follow a prescribed form, which is subject to the approval of the Queen, and announcements of changes in the wording are issued from Buckingham Palace as they occur.

Only two loyal toasts are at present authorized. These are:

(*a*) The Queen.

(*b*) The other members of the Royal Family.

The former loyal toast is, of course, unchanging. In the second, however, certain members of the Royal Family are mentioned by name, for example, the Queen Mother, the heir to the throne, etc.—and thus the form is affected by Royal Births, Marriages and Deaths, although changes are not necessarily made immediately after such events occur. This toast is not commonly proposed; but, if it is given, it is the Chairman's duty to ascertain in advance the correct current form.

As has already been stated, the proposer of a loyal toast is not required to make a speech. He simply rises and says:

(*a*) Gentlemen (or Ladies and Gentlemen),—the Queen!

The form of proposing the second loyal toast may be slightly varied, as:

(*b*) Gentlemen (or Ladies and Gentlemen),—I have the honour to propose the toast of the Duke of Edinburgh and the other members of the Royal Family.

NOTE.—For the sake of brevity the term "Gentlemen" will be used for the form of address throughout these specimen speeches, except where the context clearly demands a different wording. If ladies are present, of course the form should be amended to "Ladies and Gentlemen." If persons of title or other distinction are present, the correct form of address is in the following sequence: Your Royal Highness (if a Prince of the Blood Royal is present), Mr. Chairman (My Lord Chairman if he is a peer, or Sir Richard, etc., if a baronet or knight), Your Excellency (if an Ambassador is present), My Lords, Ladies and Gentlemen.

2. H.M. FORCES

Generally proposed by the Chairman

Gentlemen,—

It might seem incongruous that a peace-loving citizen, like myself, should now rise and ask a peace-loving company, like yourselves, to drink the health of those whose professed trade is war. We in Britain are men of peace. We hate war, and all that it means. For us the word conjures up no visions of glory, no glamour, no false heroics. We would never start a war ourselves; and we would go—as we have gone in the past—to every possible length to avert one if another nation should threaten to use force against us or against any other peace-loving country.

But as we hate war, so we love freedom, and justice; and it has happened in the past that these things so dear to us could be preserved only if they were defended by force of arms. It may happen again. It is a sombre thought, but one that must be faced. We shall do everything in our power to avert such a catastrophe; and the surest way to keep the world's peace is for us, and all other peace-loving nations, to remain strong.

That is why we have to keep up our armed forces. That is why I can, with a clear conscience and a willing heart, propose this toast. Our sailors, soldiers, and airmen do not want war any more than the civilian population. But they are always prepared for it. The price of peace, as of liberty, is eternal vigilance; and the reason why we can sleep peacefully at night is because we know that our island home is protected by men who are ready, if need be, to defend it with their lives.

We are honoured this evening with the presence of many gallant and distinguished officers of the Services. It is my privilege and pleasure to call upon three of them to respond: ———— ————, of the Royal Navy; ———— ————, of the Army; and ———— ————, of the Royal Air Force. Gentlemen, I give you the toast of Her Majesty's Forces, coupled with the names of these three officers.

Replies to the Foregoing

3. REPLY ON BEHALF OF THE ROYAL NAVY

Mr. Chairman, Gentlemen,—

On behalf of the Royal Navy, I have to return thanks to you for the very cordial manner in which this toast has been received, and for the kind way in which my name has been associated with it. I only wish that this honour had gone to someone better qualified to speak for the Service—and, indeed, I am keenly conscious that there are here this evening many of my fellow officers who are far more truly representative of the Navy than I am.

In modern times naval warfare has undergone a revolution. The old oaken vessels survive only in museums. In their place are gleaming, streamlined ships of steel. Science, friend and foe, has alternately harassed us with fiendish attacks and come to our aid with new means of defence. With these changes our system of training has had to undergo a parallel revolution, and the sailor of to-day is a highly skilled technician. Yet, fundamentally, the Navy has not changed. The spirit of the Service lies not in the ships but in the men—and not in the men's technical skill but in their hearts. Our very survival depends upon our ability to keep abreast of fast-moving modern scientific development, and there is no room for traditionalism in the materials of naval warfare; but the tradition in the Navy itself, in the hearts of the men who *are* the Navy, is timeless.

On behalf of the men of the Royal Navy, I thank you for the most cordial welcome you have given to this toast.

4. REPLY ON BEHALF OF THE ARMY

Mr. Chairman, Gentlemen,—

You have done me the great honour of associating my name with this toast. I wish I were more worthy of it, but I at least can claim one qualification for representing the Service. I am proud to belong to it. I am proud of our history, of our past victories against numerically superior and better-equipped enemies; I am proud of our traditions; and, above all, I am proud of our comradeship, which belongs to the past, the present, and, I am sure, the future.

In that one word "comradeship" lies the secret of the strength

7

of our Army—and, I believe, of every strong Army. The efficiency of an Army, in both attack and defence, depends primarily on morale; and morale, I submit, is just another word for comradeship.

We have, in the Army, a very high standard of discipline. The world knows this, and admires us for it. Yet there is nothing remotely brutal, or even harsh, about this discipline; for it, too, derives from comradeship, as it is expressed in the mutual respect between officers and men. The British citizen is famous for his respect for the law. He may not always like it—and, thanks to his unique freedom of speech, he may publicly criticize it, and urge his fellow-citizens to use all constitutional means to change it; but so long as it remains the law he will obey it. In the same way the soldier, brought up to the same British self-discipline, will obey an order even if he feels it is unjust, and complain afterwards, with the knowledge that his complaint will receive a fair hearing. That is the Army way.

Gentlemen, on behalf of the Army I thank you for the compliment you have paid us.

5. REPLY ON BEHALF OF THE ROYAL AIR FORCE

Mr. Chairman, Gentlemen,—

In the presence of so many distinguished officers of the two great historic Services I rise with some diffidence to return my sincere thanks for the honour you have done the Royal Air Force by receiving this toast with such enthusiasm. Our history is almost insignificant compared with that of the Navy and the Army; and I know I am expressing the feelings of the whole Service when I say that, in paying generous homage to the R.A.F., the people of this country have sometimes been inclined to overlook their equal debt to the older Services. It would be mere affectation if I were to pretend the R.A.F. is not proud of its record; but we are most proud of the part we have played in the co-ordinated defences of our country alongside the Navy and Army.

Our work is, perhaps, more spectacular, more showy, than that of the sailors and soldiers—that is all. We do not want to be singled out for special praise, but are very happy to share in the common bouquets—and brickbats—addressed to the Forces as a whole. In modern warfare co-operation among the three arms is not merely desirable; it is essential. Happily for us, it is mainly spontaneous, and there is no doubt in my mind that this fact was one of the main causes of our victory in the two world wars in which the R.A.F. has taken its place with the Navy and Army. We worked as a team; and the credit is due not to individual players, but to the team as a whole.

No one can say precisely what part the air force is destined to play in the age now dawning. Aviation, both Service and civilian, is developing rapidly. Let us hope that our aeroplanes will be used as bearers of friendship and merchandise rather than of instruments of war and hate. This should be our aim, and it is one that the Royal Air Force can help to attain; for we are constantly turning out trained and experienced men, all anxious that Britain's place shall be worthy of her reputation on sea and land. Gentlemen, I thank you.

6. THE ROYAL NAVY

Generally proposed by the Chairman

Gentlemen,—

It is with great pleasure that I rise to propose the toast of the Royal Navy, which we know under the modest soubriquet of the Silent Service. Except for those of us who live in certain coastal districts, the Navy is not only silent but invisible; but let it rest assured that it is never forgotten by us landlubbers. We are by heritage a seafaring nation, and from the wooden walls of Drake to the battleships of to-day our Navy has been our greatest national pride.

It would be slighting to our gallant Army and Air Force to suggest that the two world wars were won by the Navy; but I do not think that any soldier or airman would disagree with me when I say that we could not have won either of these wars if it had not been for the superb achievements of our Navy. We did not hear very much about the Navy during the last war, owing to the ever-increasing need for secrecy in the movements of ships; but we knew it was there, guarding our coastline, escorting our troopships, sweeping mines and hunting submarines, and keeping open the lifelines of our overseas communications. Had Nelson been alive on D-Day he would surely have acknowledged with pride that on that day every man in the British Navy did his duty.

The duties of the sailor to-day are very different from those of his ancestors at Trafalgar. Then the great wooden battleships were often grappled together, while the marines fought the foe hand to hand on the decks, or fired upon individual officers of the enemy with rifles from the masts. To-day warfare at sea, as on land, is more impersonal and scientific, and every sailor is a highly skilled technician. But he is still fundamentally a seaman; and, come what may, the same fine spirit is there—the same pluck which has ever distinguished our senior Service.

Gentlemen, I give you the toast of the Royal Navy, coupled with the name of ———.

7. THE ROYAL NAVY
Reply to the Foregoing Toast

Mr. Chairman, Gentlemen,—

You have told us that the Navy is silent; so it is, as long as it is well treated. After the hospitality you have given us to-night, and the very kind things you have said about us, it would ill become me to violate the traditions of silence which belong to our great Service.

But although we may be silent, we are, like the old lady's parrot, "devils to think," and hidden away in our minds there is no small amount of gratitude to our countrymen for their invariable kindness to our men.

As you very truly said, Mr. Chairman, there have been great changes since Nelson's day, and who knows what may be in store for the future? We love peace as much as you do; but if it is broken—then we shall again strive to live up to the trust you have placed in us.

Gentlemen, I most cordially thank you on behalf of the Royal Navy for the magnificent reception you have accorded this toast.

8. THE ROYAL NAVAL VOLUNTEER RESERVE
Generally proposed by the Chairman

Gentlemen,—

The toast I am about to propose requires few words of commendation from me. We are all proud of our Navy; and when a Briton thinks of the Navy, he automatically includes in the thought the Royal Naval Volunteer Reserve. The regular Navy is the guardian of our island in peace and in war. But our coastline is long, and our communications extend all over the world; and we could not feel fully secure without the reserve force that is always ready to join with the Navy to defend us against any aggressor.

Nothing is more honourable to our people than that there have always been men ready to give their time and energy to their country at a personal sacrifice to themselves. These men have become an essential part of the Navy. You do not need me to remind you of the part played by the R.N.V.R. in two world wars. Their record speaks for itself. They require no thanks from us, but we delight to acknowledge our debt.

I couple with the toast the name of ————. Gentlemen, the Royal Naval Volunteer Reserve.

9. THE ROYAL NAVAL VOLUNTEER RESERVE
Reply to the Foregoing Toast

Mr. Chairman, Gentlemen,—

I believe brevity is generally regarded as the soul of wit, and I may promise that I am about to make, in that sense, a witty speech, for it will be short. I am honoured to represent the Service which is so dear to my heart—and it is no exaggeration to say that every single member of the R.N.V.R. has the Service very much at heart. You have been good enough, sir, to refer to our work in wartime. We are at least a part of the Silent Service in this respect, we do not wish to boast of our deeds. I will say only that in the past we have done our best to be worthy of our brothers of the Navy, to whom sailoring is a profession; and, should duty and the country again call us, we shall again try not to let them down.

On behalf of the Royal Naval Volunteer Reserve, I thank you for the kind way in which you have received this toast.

10. THE ARMY
Generally proposed by the Chairman

Gentlemen,—

I believe it was the Duke of Wellington who, on inspecting a famous regiment, exclaimed, "I don't know what effect these men may have on the enemy, but, by Gad, they frighten me!"

I must confess to you, gentlemen, that, in the presence of such a distinguished gathering of officers as we are delighted to welcome to-night, my feelings are somewhat similar, and I anticipated the prospect of having to make a speech with a good deal of trepidation. I am forcibly reminded of those days, long since fled, when I was a raw recruit being put through my paces by an insistent but well-meaning Sergeant-Major.

But courage, which is the distinguishing mark of the soldier, is very contagious, and I take heart because long ago I discovered that official austerity is but the mask to hide the kindliest heart and the most magnificent spirit of comradeship that is to be found in the world. This is undoubtedly the secret of the devotion of the British soldier to his officers, and it also explains the great popularity of the soldier with the British public.

War is a horrible thing, and it would be idle to pretend that it brings anything but evil. Yet even out of a great mass of evil a few grains of good can emerge; and out of the wretchedness of war we have at least gleaned some fine qualities—not material things, but imponderables. In the Army men of different outlook, profession, and interests fought side by side, and grew to know and respect one another. They learned a new spirit, a spirit of comradeship bound up with a common loyalty; and when they thankfully laid aside their khaki that spirit lived on.

Gentlemen, I give you the toast of our gallant Army, at home and overseas, coupled with the name of ————.

11. THE ARMY

Reply to the Foregoing Toast

Mr. Chairman, Gentlemen,—

Every soldier appreciates the great honour of being called upon to reply for the Army, and I am deeply grateful to you, Mr. Chairman, for coupling my name with this toast. It is always a pleasure to know that so many of our countrymen look back with pride to the days when they served in Her Majesty's Forces. We are not a militarist nation, and far be it from me to urge that civilian life should be organized like a military operation. I, personally, should hate it! But I do think that the Army has something to offer to the nation in the way of ideals and behaviour. Never was a spirit of comradeship and co-operation more necessary for the nation than to-day; and I do not think that any young man who spends a short period in the Army early in life will emerge any the worse for it.

On behalf of the Army, I thank you for the kind way in which you have received this toast.

12. THE TERRITORIAL ARMY
Generally proposed by the Chairman

Gentlemen,—

The next toast is one which I know will be received with enthusiasm—that of the Territorials.

No praise which we can give can be too great for the young men who sacrifice their spare time to keeping fit and training for the service of their country. This, surely, is the highest form of patriotism. It is purely voluntary; it brings no reward, or even prospect of reward; and it involves a considerable sacrifice of leisure hours in evenings and week-ends. The least we can do is to show our appreciation—because it is for us that these young men are making this sacrifice.

Happily the Territorials know that their sacrifice is not in vain. They have a tradition that can stand comparison with that of any of the regular Services. Twice in this century they have been called upon to join the regular Army and meet the first shock of war, to keep a numerically superior enemy engaged while our full citizen army has been created and trained in the rear. Twice they have covered themselves with glory.

It is our earnest hope that there will be no third time. If it should come, however, we have the sure knowledge that the Territorials will play the same valiant part as in the past. Let us, then, honour them now.

Gentlemen, I give you the toast of the Territorial Army, coupling with it the name of ———.

13. THE TERRITORIAL ARMY
Reply to the Foregoing Toast

Mr. Chairman, Gentlemen,—

It is with great pride that I rise to reply to the toast of the Territorial Army, which you have honoured with such kindness. After our Chairman's words about us I feel rather embarrassed. It is good to know that our little efforts are appreciated, but I wonder if we really deserve such fulsome praise.

Certainly joining the Territorials involves some sacrifice. Our men have to put in a full working week, and many of them have domestic obligations as well. But the sacrifice is made willingly; and I must beg leave to disagree with the statement that we are unrewarded. Admittedly we are not paid any significant sum for the hours we give up—but there are other rewards besides money. I am thinking not so much of the camp and sports and the healthy outdoor activities, although these advantages are important enough, but rather of the spirit of friendship that binds us together. I do not think that anyone outside the Territorials can fully appreciate the strength of this spirit. There is comradeship in all the Services; but I think I can say with truth that in the Territorials it reaches its peak. The reason for this is simply that service is entirely voluntary, and so every man who joins starts off with a natural enthusiasm.

On behalf of the Territorial Army I should like to thank you, one and all, for the manner in which you have received this toast.

14. THE ROYAL AIR FORCE

Generally proposed by the Chairman

Gentlemen,—

The origins of our Navy and Army are lost in the mists of history—one might almost say of antiquity. It is difficult to say exactly when either Service actually began, and early records are disappointingly uninformative. It is a very different matter with the R.A.F. It has not got anything like such a long history of achievement as the other two Services; but the details of its birth and infancy are known to all.

It has been a true wonder child, and has grown up so quickly that it is difficult to realize how young it really is. Yet youth is still the keynote of the Service: youth, and with it daring, keenness, enthusiasm. It will get older in years; but I think and hope it will remain as young in spirit as it is to-day.

It would be insulting to the Service if I tried to refresh your memories with its glorious deeds, and in any case I am sure that you do not need any such reminders. Of all the battles in our history none will be remembered longer than the epic of the Battle of Britain, which was fought against such seemingly overwhelming odds. I would not say that the Navy and Army have nothing to compare with this; but I will say—and I am sure every sailor and soldier will agree—that they have nothing better than it.

The shape of future warfare is obscure, and we all hope that it will always remain so. One thing is certain, however. If another war comes, air power will play an even greater part than it did in the last war. The R.A.F. may have some terrible tests in store; but it will be able to meet them with confidence— and fully backed by the confidence of the people of the country.

Gentlemen, I ask you to drink the toast of the Royal Air Force, and I couple with it the name of ———.

15. THE ROYAL AIR FORCE

Reply to the Foregoing Toast

Mr. Chairman, Gentlemen,—

I greatly appreciate the honour you have paid me in associating my name with this toast. I hope you will forgive me if I take this opportunity to say a few words about the Service to which I belong—for, after all, we do not share the Navy's reputation for silence. Indeed, with our latest jet fighters you might almost call us the Noisy Service!

What I have to say concerns the less spectacular side of our Force, which I feel is so overshadowed by the heroic deeds of the flying men that it gets all too little recognition. I am not thinking only of the back-room boys in administration— although the value of their work can hardly be exaggerated; but I mean rather the ground staff, the men who get the 'planes in the air and keep them there.

We are sometimes accused of being rather showy, and I will admit that in one respect the R.A.F. has something in common with the theatre, although this is your fault rather than ours. You see only a few of us; the larger number work behind the scenes, as it were, and their efforts are apt to pass unnoticed by the audience. I can assure you, however, that they are not unnoticed by the aircrews themselves. They value the ground staff at their worth. They know what long hours are spent in getting machines ready for flight, in the monotonous but vital work of checking and maintenance, in the reduction of risk and the ensuring of the maximum degree of flying safety under all conditions. Quite literally, the ground staff hold the lives of the aircrew in their hands; and from my personal experience I cannot think of any hands in which they could be more safely entrusted.

On behalf of the Royal Air Force, I thank you.

16. THE COUNTY REGIMENT

Generally proposed by the Chairman

Gentlemen,—

It is my duty—and, may I add, my pleasure—to propose to you a toast which is closely connected with the County in which we reside. You will doubtless anticipate me in my announcement of the County Regiment, and I hope you will all fill your glasses and presently unite with me in drinking the health of (Lieut.-) Colonel ——— and the Officers and Men of the Royal ———.

It would be out of place for me to give you even a brief outline of the history of our famous Regiment, although I assure you that you would not find it dull hearing. Nor shall I repeat the details of its record in the last war, for these are well known to all of you. You will, I am sure, heartily agree with me when I say that our Regiment is composed of as fine a body of men as any Regiment in the Service.

In modern times there is a tendency towards centralization in all things, and local character—especially County character —is in danger of losing its identity. Personally I am inclined to regret this. I agree that it is right that we should think of ourselves as Britons first and as members of the County afterwards —but let us not forget the County altogether. There is room for both loyalties; indeed, they are complementary. Happily I do not think we shall forget, nor will people outside forget us, so long as the Regiment bears our name.

I ask you, Gentlemen, to show the Regiment that we are proud of it. I give you the toast of the Royal ———, coupled with the name of (Lieut.-) Colonel———.

17. THE COUNTY REGIMENT

Reply to the Foregoing Toast

Mr. Chairman, Gentlemen,—

In response to the call made upon me by my friend Mr. ———, who has so kindly proposed the toast of the ———, I rise to thank him and you for the flattering manner in which it has been brought before us and received. Gentlemen, I feel deeply grateful for the high opinion which has been expressed about the Regiment which I have the honour to command. It is true, as the Chairman has said, that County institutions are in danger of losing their identity, and I share his feelings on the subject. But I can assure you that so far as the Regiment is concerned the County will never be forgotten. Pride of the County is as strong in the Regiment as pride of the Regiment is in the County. It is, indeed, the link that binds all ranks together. We have in the Regiment an excellent body of officers, an equally fine set of N.C.O.s, and men without equal in the whole British Army; but the efficiency of the unit as a whole owes a good deal to the simple fact that we all belong to the same County. Metaphorically as well as literally, we all speak the same language.

Gentlemen, on behalf of the Royal ———, I thank you.

18. THE WOMEN'S SERVICES

Ladies and Gentlemen,—

I am very happy to have the privilege of proposing the toast of—well, I believe the correct description is "the Women's Services"; but on this occasion, at least, I would prefer to refer to them as ladies in uniform.

For a long period of our history it was regarded as an exclusively male function to serve one's country in the Forces. The women stayed behind and kept the home fires burning. But in modern times war has become too much for the men to cope with by themselves. In this—as in almost every other sphere of life—we have had to ask the ladies to help us out.

When the first women's units were formed they were admired for their courage and enthusiasm, but not very great hopes were placed on their value to the Services. I do not think I am giving away any military secret when I say that the War Office was frankly sceptical. However, their doubts did not last for long. Right from the beginning the ladies settled down into Service life with astonishing adaptability, and by their keenness and wonderful devotion to duty they gained the esteem of the whole nation. Now, of course, we simply cannot do without them. They have become a vital part of our Forces, and the men are proud to serve beside them.

I ask you to join me in this toast, coupling with it the name of ———, and salute the gallant ladies of the Services!

19. THE WOMEN'S SERVICES

Reply to the Foregoing Toast

Mr. Chairman, Ladies and Gentlemen,—

Thank you very much for the charming way in which you have received this toast, and for the very kind words you have said about us. Women have usually had to fight for their rights in every sphere of life, but I think it only fair to say that in the matter of recognition by their male comrades they have hardly had to fight at all. Any value that the women's Services may have owes a great deal to the courtesy and co-operation that they have been so freely given by the men. More than anything, I think, we have appreciated that we have been assigned responsible jobs to do—and left to get on with them without masculine supervision.

Our pleasure has been in sharing the duties and dangers of the men whom we love. In the old days, as you have pointed out, the woman's work in time of emergency was to sit at home and write cheerful letters when she felt anything but cheerful. That, I am sure, was a much harder task than coming out and lending a hand where it was needed.

On behalf of the women's Services, I thank you.

20. THE WOMEN'S ROYAL ARMY CORPS

Ladies and Gentlemen,—

It is a very real pleasure for me to rise and propose the toast of that gallant body the Women's Royal Army Corps. No one who has served in the Army can be unaware of the sterling work done by this branch of the Forces. It was born as the Auxiliary Territorial Service; and after magnificent pioneer work in the first World War it was stood down—it was hoped, for ever. It was no fault of the women that the war to end wars did not achieve its object; and when our nation was again forced to fight for its existence, the A.T.S. was in at the beginning. I do not need to remind you of the work done by the Service during that terrible war, when the women served in the front line in the Battle of Britain. The epic of the Mixed Batteries will live in our history for ever; and the women's courage and industry in many other fields of military activity are known and appreciated by all of us.

Surely, however, the greatest tribute to the success of the A.T.S. is that after the war ended the nation found it could not do without them. They became a permanent peace-time force, with the new name of Women's Royal Army Corps. The change of name was significant. No longer were the women merely auxiliaries, assisting the men; they had won recognition as a Corps in their own right.

Ladies and gentlemen, I give you the toast of the Women's Royal Army Corps, coupling it with the name of ———.

21. THE WOMEN'S ROYAL ARMY CORPS
Reply to the Foregoing Toast

Mr. Chairman, Ladies and Gentlemen,—

I really do not know how to thank you for all the kind things you have said about us. I wish I could think we deserved them. The W.R.A.C. is proud of its name, proud of its independence as a Corps—but proud above all of being a part of the great British Army. It is thanks to the spirit of the men with whom we serve that we are able to think of ourselves in this light. Comradeship, I believe, used to be considered a masculine common noun; now it transcends the barriers of sex, to the benefit of both men and women.

We do not pretend that we can do all the Service jobs that the men can. We do not set ourselves up as their rivals in any single sphere of activity. We want to work with them, in co-operation not competition. We are content to play what must always be a comparatively small part in the work of the Army, in the knowledge that we are making our contribution to the Service as a whole. It gives us a sense of pride and joy to know that we are able to take our share in the defence of the nation.

On behalf of the Women's Royal Army Corps, I thank you for the very kind welcome you have given to this toast.

22. THE WOMEN'S ROYAL NAVAL SERVICE
Proposed by the Chairman

Ladies and Gentlemen,—

A sailor, according to tradition, is supposed to have a wife in every port. I am afraid this is one of those legends that are not borne out by the facts, although there is no knowing what sort of life the sailor of the past used to have. But the sailor of to-day has one great advantage over his ancestor: in most ports he has a large number of sisters. I think this is the way in which the relationship between the Navy and the Wrens should be considered. They are both members of one family.

Sailoring has always been a masculine occupation, and one of the drawbacks of going to sea is the lack of feminine society. But I do not want to suggest that the value of the Wrens is merely social or decorative—although they undoubtedly have these qualities as well! Every sailor knows and esteems the work done by the women's part of our great Service. We have a glorious naval history and tradition; and we rejoice that the Wrens, as if by instinct, have grasped the elusive significance of that tradition to the full, and have not only lived up to it but have added to its lustre.

I ask you to drink the toast of the Wrens, and couple with it the name of ———.

23. THE WOMEN'S ROYAL NAVAL SERVICE
Reply to the Foregoing Toast

Mr. Chairman, Ladies and Gentlemen,—

I consider it a great honour to be chosen to respond to this toast to the Wrens. Your kind remarks have gone to my heart, because what you have said finds a ready echo in the minds of all of us. Britain is by heritage a seafaring nation, and even in the past, when the men went to sea the hearts of their women-folk went with them. Service in the Wrens gives us the opportunity of active expression of our deep pride in our glorious Navy. It makes us feel that we are no longer merely applauding spectators, but actually players on the stage of our naval history. Our parts are small, and we do not want to exaggerate them. If we contribute only a little we are satisfied. The fair name of our Navy means more to us than words can tell, and working in its service is an honour of which every member of the Wrens is always conscious.

On behalf of the Wrens I thank you for your very cordial toast.

24. THE WOMEN'S ROYAL AIR FORCE

Proposed by the Chairman

Ladies and Gentlemen,—

I cannot think of any toast that I would sooner have to propose than that of the Women's Royal Air Force. It gives me the opportunity of saying what I have always wanted to give speech to: the tremendous debt owed by the R.A.F. to the women who work with us.

The duties of the aircrew, vital as they are, are only a part of the work of the R.A.F. as a whole. Before a 'plane can become airborne it has to be got ready for flying; and when it is in the air it is still, through radio, dependent upon co-operation from the land. In both these essential functions the Women's Royal Air Force performs work of the greatest value. Its members include technicians of high qualifications, and their work calls for skill and enthusiasm and unremitting effort. The R.A.F. knows its debt to these women : it is only right that the civilian population of the country should also know and recognize the grand work they are doing.

Ladies and gentlemen, it is with the greatest pleasure that I ask you to join me and drink the toast of the Women's Royal Air Force, coupling with it the name of ———.

25. THE WOMEN'S ROYAL AIR FORCE

Reply to the Foregoing Toast

Mr. Chairman, Ladies and Gentlemen,—

On behalf of the Women's Royal Air Force I express my sincere thanks for the wonderful reception you have given to this toast. The R.A.F. rightly enjoys the admiration of the whole nation, and it is a source of great pride to us women to know that to some small extent we share in carrying on the work of this great Service. This fact is, indeed, a constant spur to us. We have a high ideal to live up to, and we try to remember always that keeping up the name of the R.A.F. is partly our responsibility. No doubt we have our faults and failings; but I do not think that these include want of zeal or of enthusiasm.

Whatever the quality of our work, it will always be the best of which we are capable.

On behalf of the Women's Royal Air Force I thank you most heartily.

26. THE NURSING SERVICES
Proposed by the Chairman

Ladies and Gentlemen,—

I am very happy to have the honour of proposing the toast of our Nursing Services. I shall not presume to tell in detail of their great work. To do them justice would take too long, and in any case I do not think that anyone is unaware of their record.

Nursing, surely, is service in the highest form. It demands unselfishness and great personal sacrifice, hard work for little reward, and a genuine humanitarian idealism. Our nurses are the nation's anonymous heroes. In peace and in war, the spirit of the Lady with the Lamp is faithfully carried on. Let us always honour them, for we can never fully repay our debt to them.

Ladies and gentlemen, I ask you to drink the toast of the Nursing Services.

27. THE NURSING SERVICES
Reply to the Foregoing Toast

Mr. Chairman, Ladies and Gentlemen,—

On behalf of the Nursing Services I wish to express my thanks for the welcome you have given to this toast, and for the kind things you have said about us. Nursing, as you have remarked, demands hard work. It demands also patience and good temper and a sense of humour—and in this I think, lies its attraction for us. In the world to-day there are many so-called ideals of doubtful value; and it is a source of happiness to us to know that ours is an ideal that can be served whole-heartedly without any doubts as to its value. That is why nurses are generally cheerful; for there is nothing in life so enjoyable as trying to help others and to do a little good in the world.

CHAPTER XII

COMMONWEALTH AND FOREIGN COUNTRIES

28. OUR AUSTRALIAN GUESTS

Ladies and Gentlemen,—

It is my very delightful duty to propose the health of our guests from the Commonwealth of Australia. We speak to-day not of the British Empire, but of the Commonwealth; and it is significant that this word was used by the Australians to describe their own country a long time back in our Imperial history. It is our pride that the nations of the Commonwealth are all governed on democratic lines; and nowhere is there a finer example of practical democracy than in Australia.

The Australians and the English spring from a common stock, and have many things in common besides language. We each have, also, some individual characteristics, and it is right that these should be equally cherished. What has always struck me as the most outstanding national characteristic of the Australians is that they all seem to be natural democrats. They never have any "side." They seem equally at home in all sorts of company, and have the happy knack of making others feel at home with them.

No speech about the Australians would be complete without some reference to that bone of contention which our two nations have been gnawing for so many years. If all contention were carried on as amicably as our Test Matches, the world would be a happier place. The symbolical significance of the Ashes is not confined to the sports ground: it represents a very real bond between the young Commonwealth of Australia and old England.

Ladies and gentlemen, I ask you to drink the toast of Our Australian Guests.

29. OUR CANADIAN GUESTS

Ladies and Gentlemen,—

In submitting to you the toast of "Our Canadian Guests," I feel that we are on common ground in such a gathering as the present, for some of us are proud to own ourselves its children

—citizens of no mean country, while others are doubtless related to it by bonds of business, if not of blood. It is true we are divided by the vast Atlantic, but the great ocean can make little difference when there exists the great union of determination to walk along the same road of progress, social uplift and commercial prosperity. We have long trod this road together, it is consecrated by our common blood, its milestones are the gravestones of our Dead, but we believe its goal is the increased happiness and betterment of our Commonwealth and of the World. I must resist the temptation to dwell on these themes, however. Rather would I, to-night, dilate on the marvellous beauties of the land, the praises of which are sung by everyone who is lucky enough to visit it. Mother Nature has bestowed on the country pine-clad mountains and smiling rivers and boundless fields and prairies. Canada's wealth in minerals no man can estimate, and her fruit and her dairy produce are literally familiar in our mouths as household words. The Canadians believe in the man and the woman who can work for the common good, and these are the guests that are always welcome, and of whom it may be truthfully said, "The more, the merrier." I may, indeed, be allowed to adapt to Canada the lines which a poet wrote about another part of the Commonwealth, because they are equally true of the Dominion :

> It's a world of wonders, Molly,
>   A world without a peer !
> And what it has, and what it wants,
>   We've nothing like it here;
> But of all its wondrous things, Molly,
>   The strangest thing to me
> Is that there the working man's the man
>   Gets first to the top of the tree.

I would not weaken the force of these lines by further comment, but ask you to raise your glasses to "Our Canadian Guests" and the Maple Leaf for Ever !

30. OUR NEW ZEALAND GUESTS

Ladies and Gentlemen,—

It is with the greatest pleasure that I rise to give you a toast which I am sure you will welcome most enthusiastically—that of Our New Zealand Guests. To us on the other side of the world, New Zealand, too often, seems merely a part of Australia; we do not realize the width of water that divides them, nor the difference in outlook of their people. But war is a great schoolmaster, and we hope that the thousands of young New Zealanders who so gallantly served together with the soldiers of the old Country do not love her any the less for having seen her and fought with her. I am certain that we here learned to love them, and even after these years most of us have maintained across the world friendships and ties contracted during that period.

Our Guests are from a wonderful country, where almost every climate and every type of vegetation known to the world can be found : from the temperate conditions of Northern Europe in the South to the almost tropical climate and features of Auckland in the North. Gentlemen, I ask you to fill your glasses and drink the toast of Our New Zealand Guests.

31. OUR INDIAN GUESTS

Ladies and Gentlemen,—

I rise to propose this toast with especial pride. The sturdy independence of our Indian friends is a quality which every Englishman can value; we see in it a repetition of those sterling virtues which we like to feel we also possess. There has always been this subconscious link between our countries, and throughout many unfortunate misunderstandings Britons could scarce forbear to admire the pluck and skill of their valiant opponents. But these dark clouds have long since been swept away, and my only excuse for such an allusion to-night is that such a background only increases the radiancy of that bright jewel of loyalty which India has ever since presented to our common Sovereign. It is not the cheap and flashy loyalty of words alone, but it has been cemented by the blood of our sons shed freely for our common ideals and our common faith. Set on such foundations, the Commonwealth must flourish : and we who have stood together in war are at one in our firm determination to make the Commonwealth the bulwark of peace and sane democracy.

We at home are staggered by the potentialities of what visitors invariably describe as "your wonderful country." The beauty and variety of its scenery are things which too many of us can sigh for but never experience. Your soil is now yielding the raw materials of industry, and what is no less precious, corn and luscious fruits. From your forests come the tiger's skin of the strong man. Surely here is Aladdin's Cave, and here resides that Genie of the Magic Lamp we lost in childhood.

My friends, that you have left this splendid land of yours and have come to visit us under the cold grey skies of old England, is a tribute we can never repay, we can but rise and drink your health with the heartiness it deserves.

32. REPLY TO THE TOAST OF OUR GUESTS

A Reply to any of the Foregoing

Mr. Chairman, Ladies and Gentlemen,—

It has been well said that he little England loves who only England knows, and it may be that some of us who come from the Dominions really have a greater insight into the greatness of the Motherland than Britons themselves.

We have long ceased to be Colonies : most of our people have never been to Europe and are proud of their independence under the British Flag. But one and all we think of old England as "Home" and we dream of the old-time villages far away where our ancestors lived, the fields they tilled and the quiet churchyard where they rest. But we don't want to make you home folks conceited, and so I must tell you some of the other side as well. Quite frankly, you seem a bit old-fashioned to us : your methods of farming and stock-rearing would be quite inadequate in our vast territories. But we do realize that the Old Country has been the pioneer, and we have followed where you have led and benefited by your experience and your mistakes.

As you say, we stand for a strong, self-supporting Commonwealth. This is no place to enter on the thorny question of tariffs; it is not such a simple question for you as some of our people imagine, and it would not be proper for the daughter to dictate to the mother. Let us try to obtain greater unity and understanding than ever before, and while we study your great problems, we know that you are not without understanding of our racial and colour question.

The sentiments so ably expressed by our Chairman to-night are, I believe, echoed by the whole Commonwealth and are themselves the strongest guarantees of the greatness which the future holds in store for our Commonwealth. We have no selfish desires for our own well-being apart from that of the general prosperity of the English-speaking race.

Ladies and gentlemen, I thank you.

33. OUR FOREIGN GUESTS

A typical example

Gentlemen,—

It is my privilege to extend a formal welcome to our guests from the United States of America. Technically, I believe, your status in this country goes under the heading of aliens. In fact, I cannot think of any word less suitable either as a description of yourselves or as an expression of our feelings towards you. I ask you, therefore, to make yourselves at home for as long as you choose to remain in our country. We are happy to see you here, and hope that your stay will be a pleasant one.

It has been said that the reason for the close bond between the American and British peoples is that we speak a common language. I do not personally subscribe to this opinion: not because the language is *not* common (although a good case could be made out for that point of view), but because I think our association goes a good deal deeper. Certainly it depends upon some common factor: and I think this is to be found in the similarity in our ways of life.

The American way is not always the British way. On many things we agree to differ. But fundamentally we base our conduct on the same principles, the same ideals of freedom and justice and equality of opportunity.

We, in Britain, shall never forget the two World Wars in which we fought side by side with the Americans. In these bitter and brutal conflicts our friendship was put to a supreme test, and it emerged stronger than ever. When the G.I.s invaded England they gave us a new understanding of the American people; and we hope that they took away with them some pleasant memories of our own folk. On D-Day, G.I.s and Tommies crossed the Channel together, serving under a unified command, with a degree of co-operation never before achieved between two independent nations.

A few people, on both sides of the Atlantic, have sought to work out a profit-and-loss account on the war in favour of one country or the other. I do not think this attitude is typical of the common people of either of our two countries. Victory and peace were achieved above all by the unity of our effort. We are, however, conscious of one very great debt to you. After the Second World War, when many of our cities bore ugly scars, and our economic life was in jeopardy, you afforded us the considerable assistance that made our reconstruction possible. For this generosity we can never thank you sufficiently.

Gentlemen, I ask you to rise and drink the health of our welcome guests from the great United States of America.

CHAPTER XIII

ECCLESIASTICAL

34. THE CHURCH AND HER DIGNITARIES

The Dedication of a Church[1]

Gentlemen,—

It is a privilege to address you on this memorable day, the day which we have all prayed and worked for so long, when our Church, at last completed, has been opened and dedicated by our Bishop.

It is indeed a matter of thanksgiving that our Church has given up the old conservative policy of merely clinging to what she has got: so often in our villages the old Parish Church stands, long ago forsaken by the people who have moved to a new site a mile or so away, or have even migrated into the great industrial areas. To-day the Church must push out to new ground to seek and reclaim her children.

It is, therefore, a great joy that in this rapidly growing district we have been able to build a Church that is not unworthy of the sacred use for which it is designed. Foremost, of course, it must ever be the House of Prayer, but may we not also hope that this Church will become the centre of a healthy and Christian society, giving meaning and purpose to the daily round of labour and recreation which is the lot of most of us?

It has not been, I know full well, without severe self-denial and arduous labour that this edifice has been erected, but it is this very fact that makes our joy. We are not giving what has cost us nothing. We believe that our dedication to-day is only the beginning of that continuous consecration of this building by the service and prayers of ourselves and of generations yet unborn.

[1] This speech can be adapted for use at the laying of the foundation-stone of a church.

35. OUR BISHOP, MODERATOR OR PRESIDENT

Proposed by the Chairman at a Dinner or Meeting

Gentlemen,—

The toast I have to propose is that of the Bishop of this Diocese. I often think that it is the misfortune of laymen like ourselves that we see so little of our Bishops, but we realize that they are men of vast activities, and the burden of our present enormous diocese naturally prevents them from devoting too much time to any particular parish. Labouring under the disadvantage of overwork, it is gratifying to realize in what high regard our Bishops are held by the community. Their wisdom and insight are rightly monopolized by the great questions arising from the general conduct and guidance of the Church. But what may be the gain of the Church as a whole is our individual loss, and a Bishop remains somewhat of a mystery to ordinary Churchpeople, although we revere his great office. Their discipline is based upon the love and reverence which we feel towards them, and by the respect which every Churchman owes to their holy office.

We are delighted to have our own good Bishop among us to-day : only a few of us can have any idea of all he does for us. Whether he is dealing with the rich and exalted or with the humblest and the poor, our Bishop is the true Father in God, ever ready to share their joys or help in their sorrows. The day that anyone makes his acquaintance is always a memorable one in his life and there are few who leave that gracious and venerable presence without feeling inspired and encouraged. Gentlemen, I give you the toast of Our Bishop.

36. THE CLERGY

Proposed by the Chairman at a County Dinner

Gentlemen,—

There is, I am sure, no toast more welcome to those I see before me this evening than that I am about to propose— namely, the health of our respected Bishop and of the Clergy of this Diocese. Of the latter I see a goodly sprinkling, and it is with satisfaction that we note the presence of so many of our clergy at social gatherings and meetings in our county, convinced as we are that both we and the Church have much to gain from the intimacy so engendered between them and those under their spiritual charge. As a body of men they commend themselves highly to our friendship, as ministers of religion they have proved themselves able exponents of its truth. Gentlemen, the Bishop and his Clergy.

37. THE VICAR

Proposed by a Churchwarden at a Dinner of the Parochial Council

Gentlemen,—

It is my very great pleasure to propose the health of our Vicar. We often hear from the pulpit what our Vicar thinks of us, but this is one of the rare occasions when we can tell him what we think of him. The only difficulty I feel in doing so is that perfect candour might place too great a strain upon his modesty. Truly he is our "Parson," and I like to use that old-fashioned word, meaning as it does "The Person" of the parish around whom all the religious and social activities of the place centre. He is the person who represents our parish to the outsider, and also, as the friend and confidant of us all, he is able to unite us in the strong bonds of friendship and understanding.

Such a man we know our Vicar is, but his quiet and unostentatious manner often makes it difficult to appreciate to the full the splendid work he is doing. I know I am only voicing the sentiments of every member of our Council in telling the Vicar that we laymen not only sympathise with him in his work, but are anxious to assist him practically. This can be done in many ways, but one of the most important is in the realm of finance: by relieving the Clergy of the financial anxiety that, I fear, is too often their lot, and by contributing according to our ability to the funds of our Church. Although we shall drink our Vicar's health with the enthusiasm it deserves, let us not forget that there are more practical ways of showing our appreciation.

Gentlemen,—Our "Parson."

38. THE CLERGY AND MINISTERS OF ALL DENOMINATIONS

Proposed at a Public Dinner

Gentlemen,—

To all Christians, whatever their creed may be, the toast which I have to propose must be an acceptable one—it is the Clergy and Ministers of all Religious Denominations.

The time is now past when those of different creeds, if not actually striving the one against the other, were at least highly antagonistic; nowadays, despite differences of doctrine and practice, all creeds are working together for one common end, the bettering of humanity; the fight is the same fight, though the weapons may be different. It is for this reason that this collective toast is a most proper one.

The work of our clergy and ministers demands a thorough knowledge of their fellow-men, ability, and self-sacrifice, and of these, we are happy to think, no single denomination has a monopoly. One cannot help feeling, too, that occasions like this, when ministers of different creeds meet together unprofessionally, so to speak, have done much to foster the spirit of toleration and mutual understanding which is so marked in the Christianity of to-day, and that therefore we have good reason to give them a hearty welcome. It is as fellow labourers in the Lord's vineyard that I call upon you to toast them—the Clergy and Ministers of all Denominations, coupled with the names of the Rev. Mr. —— and the Rev. Mr. ——.

39. THE ARMY PADRE OR SCHOOL CHAPLAIN

Gentlemen,—

I know this is going to be a popular toast, so I shall delay it for as short a time as possible. Moreover, I do not want to embarrass the subject of the toast, who is without doubt the most modest man in this company. He has devoted his life to the ideal of doing good, and nothing delights him more than doing good by stealth. We honour him for the good deeds that we know he has committed; but I am sure that these are only a fraction of the good works he has done without being found out. He is our guide, philosopher, and friend. We take our troubles to him, knowing that we shall always get sympathy and sound advice.

Gentlemen, I give you the toast of our Padre (Chaplain).

CHAPTER XIV

THE LEGISLATURE

40. THE HOUSE OF COMMONS

My Lords and Gentlemen,—

In asking you to honour the toast of the House of Commons I ask you to honour an institution of which we are as a nation proud. There is no other similar institution in the world where perfect freedom of debate is so seldom marred by lack of dignity or want of good taste, and as it is composed of representatives of the people so it is itself representative of the best traditions of our national character and demeanour. It would, no doubt, be a comparatively easy task for any theorist to prepare a strong indictment of our existing Parliamentary system; it is very easy to say that the Commons talk too much and do too little, and that the Lords are an anachronism that should be swept away. But, apart from theory and Utopian schemes, I venture to think that the Mother of Parliaments is still in enjoyment of a vigorous and useful vitality, and is as a whole still capable of transacting effectually the business of the country. There are periods of congestion, no doubt, and occasionally recurring periods of obstruction, but the work is done and well done—and after all that is the best thing one can say of any working assembly. It is a pleasure to us to welcome here tonight a distinguished Member of Parliament, whose name I am permitted to couple with this toast. The Hon. Member for —— enjoys a high reputation far beyond the bounds of his own constituency, and requires no introduction from me. As you know, he is a man who has many calls upon his time, and I should like to take this opportunity of telling him how much we appreciate his presence among us to-night. I will not detain you longer, but give you the toast of the House of Commons, coupled with the name of the Hon. Member for ——, ——.

41. HER MAJESTY'S MINISTERS

Proposed by the Chairman

My Lords and Gentlemen,—

From men who pursue their peaceful way aloof from the storm and turmoil of political life, a deep debt is due to those who, casting their lot on that troubled sea, guide, in the Sovereign's name, the ship of State. A warm sense of that debt is expressed in the toast I now offer to you—"The Health of Her Majesty's Ministers." One of the outstanding facts in our national history is the almost inexhaustible supply of men of high integrity and fine calibre, competent to guide and represent so old and great a Power. However large one individual statesman may loom upon the stage, however rich and varied his gifts may be, however strong and dynamic his personality, however compelling his will, steadfast his purpose, rich his resources,—when his part has been played, his final exit made, and his voice and figure are heard and seen no more, the nation has never yet been forced to confess that he is irreplaceable. When Lord Beaconsfield died, when Mr. Gladstone died, it seemed impossible that the world could go on unmoved, or that anyone could be found to discharge their great functions with the same dignity and skill. So it has been before, and so it will be again. We look at the vacant chair wondering who can be found to fill it, and still our race continues to produce worthy successors to those who have passed into history. The position of a minister is one of great dignity and high honour, but his life is by no means an easy one; so great are his responsibilities, so incessant are the demands on his mental and physical energy that one cannot help feeling that the sacrifice he makes of private ease and leisure is a very great one. He is constantly at the beck and call of his country and can never be certain that the plans he has made for his all-too-scarce leisure moments will not be destroyed by the call of duty. His is a thankless position, for whatever his actions, whatever his words, they will be heavily criticized by one party or another. We are lucky indeed to have so many men patriotic enough to give their services to the Crown and strong enough in character and physique to stand the heavy strain that is the inevitable lot of a Minister of the Crown. We are honoured with the presence here to-night of one of the Nation's Councillors, so with the

Health of Her Majesty's Ministers I would couple the name of the Right Honourable ——.

42. THE COUNTY MEMBERS

Proposed by the Chairman at a Dinner to them

Gentlemen,—

I have now come to the toast of the evening, and I must ask you all to fill your glasses so as to do full honour to the toast— "Our County Members." We have had a stormy session, and after the turmoil and worry of Parliament our Members have come among us to give us an account of their stewardship. I think we are all agreed that the stewardship they hold should not be exchanged for that of the "Chiltern Hundreds." We have noticed, and we shall always, I may add, continue to notice, all that goes on in Parliament; but when we entrusted our interests to Messrs. —— and ——, we did so in full and entire confidence—a confidence which has never been betrayed. Not only that, but we believe that our representatives have the welfare of the community at heart. That they have the welfare of us, their fellow-townsmen and fellow-countrymen at heart, we are satisfied. They have watched over us; they have come amongst us on several occasions lately, and shown the interest they take in our schools and in our sports, in our various manufactures and in our holidays. They have gained our votes, and we trust they will long live to represent the old County in Parliament. I might say a great deal more respecting our representatives, socially and politically, but their acts are patent to us all, and you will, I am sure, endorse the proposal I have to make and drink their health, with all the honours. Gentlemen, I give you the toast of the Members for the County of ——.

43. PROPOSING A CANDIDATE FOR ELECTION

By the Chairman of the Meeting

Gentlemen,—

I think it is very appropriate that the lot should have fallen to me to introduce my very old friend Mr. —— to you as the Parliamentary Candidate for this Borough.

I have not come here to tell you of his brilliant 'Varsity record, or of his success, which has surprised none of his friends, in his profession (trade). I have come rather to bear testimony to his sterling qualities as a man. It is said you should always play golf with a lady before you propose to her, for that is the best and quickest way of proving character.

Gentlemen, I have tried this test with your Candidate, and I assure you he has not been found wanting though heavily handicapped. We have also met under the more fiery ordeal of battle. I know him as a real man, and though, I tell you as a deep secret, I do not always agree with all he says, yet I have long found that his wide sympathies and many interests are greater than any rigid, hide-bound party dogmas. He is a candidate of whom any constituency may be proud; in fact, he is one of the best, as you will all realize before any of you are much older. It is the personal element that wins elections, and the Party is to be congratulated on having put forward such an admirable candidate. When he becomes your Member, as I am confident he will, I know you will have every reason to be delighted with the choice you have made.

CHAPTER XV

LEGAL

44. HER MAJESTY'S JUDGES

Gentlemen,—

The honour of proposing the health of Her Majesty's Judges has been placed upon me, and the thought of the many eloquent speeches which are daily addressed to our learned and distinguished guests by the most accomplished speakers of the land is one that troubles me not a little.

An American visitor recently told me that he regarded two of our institutions as being typical of the English character: our Cathedrals and the Zoological Gardens. I believe he would have been more correct if he had said Her Majesty's Judges, and indeed they combine in themselves the popularity and the comprehensiveness of the one with the dignity and venerability of the other. I have, as a matter of fact, heard the same learned Judge described in the same week as a saint and also as an old tiger—but perhaps I am betraying confidences!

The secret of the respect in which we hold our Judges is not in their robes or in their ceremony which surrounds their office, but in the fact that we feel they possess in a signal degree what many of us most covet, and all of us admire—an open mind.

It must be a stupendously difficult task to banish from the mind the natural prejudices to which human nature is prone, and reserve any decision until the last tittle of evidence has been given—to bear in mind the cogent arguments of the plaintiff, while watching the slowly rising structure of a convincing defence. I am told that even the most eminent occupants of the Bench have found this no easy task; it is indeed a quality which takes years of labour to reach its full maturity.

I am very glad that the name of Mr. Justice —— has been coupled with this toast; to his wisdom and courtesy Mr. Justice of the other. I have, as a matter of fact, heard the same learned Judge described in the same week as a saint and also as an old the whole Court is radiated by his personality and charm: everyone feels that his work, however humble and insignificant, is not without its bearing on his deliberations: that may be the reason that the learned Judge gets the best out of everybody, for he inspires them with some of his own genius. Litigants leave his court, not always glad, but invariably feeling that right and common sense have prevailed.

I must not say more of our learned guest, for I feel I may already have committed some indiscretion, which may possibly amount to a felony, or even high treason when committed in the presence of a Judge. I sincerely hope that Mr. Justice —— will not assume the Black Cap forthwith and sentence me to the penalty, I have no doubt, you will think just.

Gentlemen, etc.

45. THE LORD-LIEUTENANT OF THE COUNTY

Proposed by the Chairman

Gentlemen,—

Next to the Loyal toasts which you have honoured, I have to propose the health of the Lord-Lieutenant of this County, —— ——. It is scarcely necessary for me to assure him of the estimation in which he is held. We who live in the neighbourhood hear much of his kindness and benevolence, and of the manner in which he performs the duties of landlord and neighbour, duties not merely social and not easy of accomplishment, so as to please, as he does, all with whom he comes in contact. Suffice it to say that all our experience of him leads us to wish him many more years in the exalted position he now holds. Gentlemen, let us drink Long Life and Happiness to the Lord-Lieutenant, who by his influence and energy has done so much for the County and those living in it. The Health of the Lord-Lieutenant of the County of ——.

46. THE MAGISTRATES

Gentlemen,—

It is my privilege to-day to propose the health of the Magistrates of the County and Borough of ——; and while I gladly comply with the request made of me, I cannot help expressing a wish that the task had fallen to other hands, and a more practised tongue. Fortunately, however, what I have to say has

been no doubt anticipated by you all. We here are all aware of
the estimation in which the Magistrates are held, the general
satisfaction with which their decisions are acknowledged, and
the manner in which they devote themselves to a thankless
office. Their position lays them peculiarly open to criticism, but
I am sure that all must recognize their fairness and impartiality,
and if sometimes higher courts hold that they have erred, these
errors are due to the complexity of the law, not to any bias on
their part. Those gentlemen who have undertaken the administration of our laws are well known to you all; they have served
the State before, they have done much good in their generation;
and their present work is one that is of the highest importance
to the State and all its citizens. Socially and officially we regard
them with goodwill and respect. Let us drink their healths in
a bumper. "The Magistrates of the County of—— and the
Borough of——."

47. REPLY BY ONE OF THE MAGISTRATES

Gentlemen,—

As the hour is getting late I will not long detain you. I have
to thank you, Sir, and this distinguished company for the very
kind way in which the toast of the Magistrates has been proposed and received. After some years on the bench it becomes,
I find, a comparatively easy matter in most cases to determine
whether or not the accused is guilty. The difficulty begins when
an accused has been found guilty and we have to make up our
minds what to do with him. We have always endeavoured to
bear in mind that justice is kind and the quality of mercy must
not be strained. You may depend upon it that, although hard
cases may occasionally crop up, the general tendency through
the length and breadth of the land is not on the side of severity
but of leniency. We do not forget that mercy is the true inter-
preter of justice, but there are cases wher mercy would be mis-
interpreted as fear and would conseque ly be misplaced. A
suitable severity frequently prevents crime. The law is only a
terror for evil-doers; no honest citizen need fear it, and therefore, when it is necessary to put the law in force with severity,
it is presupposed that the offender is not an honest citizen, but
an old hand upon whom leniency would be wasted. On the
other side there are many cases when leniency is true mercy,
when a caution will suffice to prevent a repetition oi the offence.

So when you hear of "Justices' justice," put yourself in their place, hear the evidence in the mass and then decide for yourselves whether, knowing all they know, you would not have done the same. Gentlemen, I will not detain you longer. Once more I thank you very heartily for the manner in which you have received this toast.

CHAPTER XVI

SOCIAL TOASTS

WEDDINGS—CHRISTENINGS—BIRTHDAYS—DINNERS

48. THE BRIDE AND BRIDEGROOM

Proposed by an Old Friend of the Bride

I believe that the custom of making speeches at wedding festivities is going out of fashion, but I am sure that there are many present on this happy occasion who will pardon, and perhaps expect a few words from one like myself who has known and greatly esteemed both Bride and Bridegroom from their childhood. This drinking of health, with its pretty touch of romance, seems to me specially appropriate in the case of the charming couple to-day.

Let us, therefore, raise our glasses to the Bride and Bridegroom, wishing, as we do from our hearts, that health, happiness, and prosperity may attend them through long years of a married life, graced by the sunlight of a lasting love. May the affection which animates them to-day burn brighter and more steadfastly as time rolls on, so that all of us who have the privilege of being here to-day may be glad in after-years to remember that we assisted at the opening of a happy story of married life.

I can remember the Bride in her sweet and sunny girlhood, and should like to be allowed to say of her, in the words, slightly altered, of Robert Burns:

> "I see her in the dewy flowers,
>   I see her sweet and fair;
> I hear her in the tuneful birds,
>   I hear her charm the air.
> There's not a bonnie flower that springs
>   In all the countryside,
> There's not a bonnie bird that sings
>   But minds me of the Bride."

But before I sit down I am tempted to say a few words about the Wedding Ring which has played so important a part in to-day's ceremony:

"And as that ring is rarely found
To flaw or else to sever,
So may their love as endless prove,
And pure as gold for ever."

Ladies and gentlemen, "The Bride and Bridegroom."

49. ANOTHER ON A SIMILAR OCCASION

Ladies and Gentlemen,—

It is my privilege to ask you to honour the toast of the day —the Bride and Bridegroom. If a long acquaintance with the young people who have this morning cast in their lot together can constitute a right to propose their health and prosperity, I certainly have a claim. I have known them pretty well all their young lives, and no one rejoices more truly than I do to see their happiness thus assured. They love each other wisely and well. They have every prospect of true happiness—the love and regard of a very large circle of friends, and a sufficiency of worldly goods. We wish them a long and happy life, with silver and golden wedding-days in store for them, surrounded by those they love. Ladies and gentlemen, I need not insist upon your responding heartily to the toast, since you all feel as I do. May every blessing and happiness attend the Bride and Bridegroom, and long life to them!

50. RESPONSE OF THE BRIDEGROOM

Mr. ——, and Ladies and Gentlemen,—

My wife and I are, quite happily, beginning our wedded life by starting with an agreement—the agreement being our most grateful thanks to you, Mr. ——, for the very kind and pleasant manner in which you have proposed our health, and to you all for the hearty manner in which you have responded to the good wishes so eloquently expressed by our friend.

I do not deserve all the good things that have been said of me, but I will try to deserve them, and to be worthy of my wife.

In conclusion let me again say that I greatly appreciate your kindness, and my wife—you see I am getting used to her new title—wishes me to thank you most heartily for your good wishes. I am sincerely grateful to you all for your kindness in so cheerily drinking our health.

51. REPLY BY THE BRIDEGROOM, INCLUDING THE TOAST OF THE BRIDESMAIDS

Ladies and Gentlemen,—

I thank you very earnestly for the heartiness with which the toast of my wife and myself has been proposed and received to-day, and for your generous good wishes for our happiness. I am sure that *I* shall be happy, and I shall make it my life's highest purpose to make the future for my wife a succession of years of joy and happiness. Please be assured how very deeply and gratefully we thank you. But before I sit down I have the very pleasant duty of proposing to you a toast. There are some ladies here to whom my wife is greatly indebted for the skill with which they helped her to dress this morning. I mean, of course, the Bridesmaids. Quite apart from the very capable manner in which they have discharged their duties, we are all delighted to be honoured with their presence to-day. In my wife's name and my own I thank them for their attention, for the success won by their good taste and their skilful fingers.

Let me specially address the gentlemen present and express my wonder, if with such a wealth of grace and beauty around them they can possibly choose to remain bachelors.

Gentlemen, I am sure you will join me in drinking to the health and "happy-day" prosperity of our charming young friends—the Bridesmaids of to-day and the Brides that should be of a speedy to-morrow.

52. RESPONSE TO THE TOAST OF THE BRIDESMAIDS

By the Best Man

Ladies and Gentlemen,—

You see before you a man who is both fortunate and unfortunate. Fortunate in being the mouthpiece of so many charming young ladies; unfortunate in being so incapable of giving due expression to their opinions and sentiments. I am sure they are all delighted to have been of use to-day, only second as ornaments to the Bride herself. I can only guess at their feelings, for I can assure you that I have never occupied so gracious and so important a position as that of a Bridesmaid;

but I can imagine that they are glad to see their friend so happily married, and are themselves prepared to follow so good an example when partners turn up after their own hearts. May they all have cause to follow Shakespeare's advice to go down on their knees and thank God, fasting, for a good man's love.

Where the eyes of mankind have been I cannot tell; but I confess it is not saying much for bachelor tastes if they permit my fair friends to be bridesmaids again. For my own part—well—I won't confess too much. Wait and see! Now with this mysterious hint I will close.

CHRISTENING PARTY

53. THE HEALTH OF THE BABY

Ladies and Gentlemen,—

It is with diffidence that I rise in the capacity of Godfather to express in the "vulgar tongue," according to my sponsorship, my feelings on behalf of the fine little fellow who has been the central figure in our ceremony to-day. Although my acquaintance with the young [gentleman] is of the slightest, I am sure he will permit me to speak of him by his Christian name, and to wish all prosperity and happiness to —— ——. With such an auspicious commencement as this has been, under the care of parents of whose friendship we are, as anyone might well be, proud—enjoying such advantages as these—his prospects will not be marred by any imperfection in my utterance of our good wishes for him. May the rosy promises of his young life be more than realized. May he long live to be a source of comfort and happiness to his parents, the companion and friend of their middle age, and the prop and stay of their declining years. It may be that successors will come to these honours of the first-born and I am sure we all most cordially wish everything for our kind host and hostess that may tend to complete their happiness. Fill your glasses, bumpers please, ladies and gentlemen, and drink with all the honours to the health and long life of —— (here mention names). God bless him!

54. REPLY TO THE FOREGOING TOAST

By the Father

Ladies and Gentlemen,—

The very hearty way in which my old friend has so kindly proposed the health of our little child demands my warmest acknowledgments, and your kindness in coming here to-day to welcome the little stranger and to cheer him upon the first stage of his existence, my wife and I accept as a great compliment and highly appreciate. I scarcely know how to thank you for all your good wishes. Many very handsome and flattering things have been said of my wife and myself which we do not deserve. But there is at any rate one point upon which I can speak, and that is the pleasure it has given us to be able to welcome you here to-day. We are always glad to see our friends, and we hope that we shall see you—if not in similar circumstances, at any rate on many other occasions. We are greatly obliged to the friends who have kindly consented to stand Sponsors for the little one, and we tender our sincere thanks to them and to you all, for your presence and presents, your company and your good wishes. Before I sit down I would ask you to drink to the Sponsors, the Godmother and the Godfathers, here to-day. Their healths and their families—may they all live long and prosper!

BIRTHDAY PARTY

55. THE HEALTH OF THE HERO OF THE DAY

Proposed by an Old Friend

Ladies and Gentlemen,—

A very pleasant duty has devolved upon me to-day, and I only regret that I cannot do the subject more justice. I have to propose to you the health of Mr. ——, and to request you to drink the toast, wishing him many happy returns of the day. As one of his oldest friends I may be permitted to say a few words concerning him, and to express to those around me the great pleasure that association with him has given me and all with whom he has come in contact. Many of us have special reasons for knowing what a good fellow he is, and all have experienced his kind hospitality and realize he is "one of the best." We recognize many present here who have grown up with our friendship, and it is a great and sure test of truth in friends when we see year after year the same smiling faces round the board. As a father, husband and friend, Mr. ⸺ has won the esteem of all who have come into contact with him, and both in his public and private life he has set a high ideal before him. Ladies and gentlemen, I am sure you want no words of mine to convince you of our friend's fine qualities, nor will I longer detain you, but at once call upon you to join me in wishing Mr. ⸺ many happy returns of his Birthday.

56. REPLY TO THE FOREGOING TOAST

Ladies and Gentlemen,—

My old friend, Mr. ⸺, has almost taken away my breath by the eulogy he has pronounced upon my unworthy self, for I am but too painfully conscious how far short I fall of the imaginary me he has conjured up for your inspection. But in one sense he is right. I am thankful to have so many kind friends, and very glad to welcome you all. I am not so young as I was, and as we begin to descend the path of life we are brought face to face with many rough steps and many obstacles which we had not noticed before. But even in these circumstances nothing is so cheering as the support of our friends; and the friendship I can fortunately lay claim to, and which I have enjoyed for so many years, is a bright light upon the road. My friend, Mr. ⸺ was kind, too kind, to give me credit for the power of retaining friends. But we must remember that as it takes two to make a quarrel, so it takes two to make a friendship. It is not a one-sided arrangement. To you, my friends, much of my happiness must be ascribed, and by your coming here to-day you have given me much pleasure. Thank you very much for your kind wishes, and I trust we may all be spared to meet here for many a year to come.

57. THE HEALTH OF A YOUNG MAN ON HIS TWENTY-FIRST BIRTHDAY

Proposed by an Old Friend

Ladies and Gentlemen,—

It is my very delightful task to propose the health of ⸺ on this his twenty-first birthday. Yesterday he was an infant, a very sturdy one perhaps—but still an infant hardly regarded by the law as existing at all. To-day he has arrived at man's estate with all its privileges, and perhaps I may add, its disadvantages, ranging as they do from a Parliamentary vote to a key of the front door—which of the two he may find the more useless I need not discuss. A twenty-first birthday seems to me to resemble the summit of a mountain : we climb up so slowly to it, and desire it so eagerly : having got there we begin to slide down, going quicker and quicker as the years fly on, and desiring more and more to be back on the top again.

Of course I should not be so foolish as to suggest that some troubles and worries do not lie ahead, but when they come —— will meet them like the fine young fellow he is, for the splendid record he has already established, both on the sportsfield and in the more serious things of life, is evidence of the sterling qualities which will carry him to triumph over everything the future may have in store for him.

I cannot pretend to foretell the future by the arts of the phrenologist or the palmist : my art of divination depends upon more reliable portents than bumps or life lines. I look rather to the fact that —— has all the true characteristics of a gentleman, by which I mean a quick and ready sympathy for the opinions and feelings of others, and a mind that has been trained to appreciate what is worth knowing and equipped with the capacity to learn it.

It is for this reason that all his many friends regard ——'s future with confidence and join in the hope, not only that prosperity and happiness may attend him, but that his life may be one of usefulness and service to his country and his friends. Gentlemen, I give you the toast of the evening ——, which we will celebrate with musical honours.

58. REPLY

Mr. ——, Ladies and Gentlemen,—

I don't profess to be much of a speaker, and I am especially at a disadvantage in having to reply to such a kind speech on such a very unworthy and uninteresting topic as myself. I could not give you very much information on the theory of the divisibility of the atom, or the hibernation of gold fishes, but I feel, after listening to the proposer of this toast, that I know much more of these obscure subjects than I do of myself.

Mr. —— has said that yesterday I was an infant, and perhaps I am too near my babyhood to realize all my early errors and precociousness; but I understand that in the future I am to assume the cloak of wisdom which distinguishes my elders and betters.   I am afraid I shall take a long time to become accustomed to such a garb, but I trust I shall not prove to be a sheep in lion's clothing.   You, sir, have referred to the future, and perhaps it is natural at twenty-one to look forward eagerly. I know there are many dangers and difficulties ahead, but I hope that, with such kind friends around me, they will only act as a spur to urge me on to better things.

Any little thing that I have done in the past is due entirely to the experience and loving wisdom of my father and mother : I owe everything to their help and devotion, and it is my greatest ambition to be worthy of them in the future.   I am determined to do my best, and the very kind things that have been said to-night will be greatly cherished throughout the years to come.

59. THE HEALTH OF A YOUNG LADY ON HER TWENTY-FIRST BIRTHDAY

Proposed by an Old Friend

Ladies and Gentlemen,—

My task this evening is a delightful one—that of proposing the health of —— on her twenty-first birthday.   I have known —— from her earliest years, and I have had few greater pleasures than that of being able to come here to-night and propose her health on this great day of her life.

I remember so well the pretty little baby, sleeping peacefully by day, and waking vocally by night; and how the little crawling mite was never more charming than when she was naughty.   Then the curly-headed little maid sitting on my knee devouring fairy stories, and rather more substantial sweetmeats as well.   Next came the schoolgirl, solving so easily the problems that have so long puzzled the ages, and poor old people like ourselves.

Now we have the woman, taking her part in the sports and pleasures of life while not forgetful of its more serious calls.   She is as kind as she is beautiful, as unassuming as she is clever; the delight of her parents, the joy of her friends.   Whatever her radiant future may be, it will never be brighter than her friends desire, or she deserves.

60. REPLY

Mr. ——, Ladies and Gentlemen,—

You must really excuse my not making a speech to-night. I want to say so much that I can't say anything at all except, Thank you, thank you, so much!

61. SPEECH FOR A SILVER WEDDING

Ladies and Gentlemen,—

My friends, I have been requested this evening to undertake a duty, which I generally take great pains to avoid—that of proposing a toast. But on this occasion I am not going to shirk, I am not even going to try, because it is such a very pleasant duty. To be asked to propose the toast of the evening is in itself an honour, but in the case of the toast I am going to give you it is more than an honour, it is a privilege which nothing but a close and life-long friendship could entitle me to claim. To-day our host and hostess are celebrating the anniversary of a singularly happy marriage and it is but fitting that, on their Silver Wedding Day, we their friends should unite to drink most heartily their health and to wish them continued happiness. With our thoughts for Mr. —— arise naturally thoughts of Mrs. ——, that good and ever-charming lady whose friendship we are proud to have, and whose kindness and courtesy are valued by us all. She has a great place in our thoughts and our esteem during this celebration of the Silver Wedding.

Time in his passing has dealt very gently with our two friends whose health I am about to propose; he has not dared to lay an unkind finger on their honoured heads. He respects them, and though he may plague less deserving mortals, he passes our host and hostess smilingly year after year.

Youthfulness, merriment, good-humour, cheerfulness, sit at their board, helping them to defy Time. "Age cannot wither nor custom stale" the infinite variety of our friends' good parts. They ward off Time's attacks and reach the Silver Wedding Day with hearts young, and faces as bright as polished silver itself, reflecting joy and happiness all around them.

So, ladies and gentlemen, "uprouse ye" merrily for the glad celebration of this Silver Wedding Day. As by the magic power of an alchemist, the silver will turn into the richer metal of a Golden Wedding Day. The springtime of life may have gone, but the smiling summer remains, and we look forward hopefully to a golden-lined autumn of their lives to come, when the harvest of good deeds shall be attended by troops of friends and loving memories.

I will now ask you to drink with me, in hearty congratulations on this anniversary, to Mr. and Mrs. ——; may health and happiness be with them now and in the future. May they have Many Happy Returns of the Day. God bless them!

62. REPLY TO TOAST OF SILVER WEDDING

By the Husband

Mr. ——, Ladies and Gentlemen,—

You will, I am sure, pity me in the position in which I find myself. I am not, of course, referring to the matrimonial state, but to the position in which I have been placed by the—as far as I am personally concerned—undeserved praises of my old friend who has so eloquently proposed my wife's health and my own.

Ladies and gentlemen, what can I say to thank you save that my wife and myself do thank you from the bottom of our hearts? For myself I must tell you that I do not deserve the praise you have lavished on us; but I may also tell you she does. No words of mine could express what for more than twenty-five years she has been to me, what help and support in the battle of life she has given me by her love, her sympathy, her tact and power of understanding; and if I have been at all successful, it is to her that the greatest part of the credit is due.

I said for "more than twenty-five years" this influence has been over me. Yes: twenty-seven years ago I first met my wife that was to be, and is! Those were happy days—happy days indeed—foreshadowing the happier ones yet to come.

Ladies and gentlemen, one and all, I thank you in the name of all my family. We are delighted to see you here, and if we are spared we hope that this will not be the last time by any means that we shall have the pleasure of seeing you at our house. We owe you another vote of thanks for your charming gifts—a kindly remembrance of our wedding-day. For these, much thanks! I am sure you will excuse my not saying more now, but you will quite understand how highly, how sincerely, my wife, my children, and myself appreciate your kind expressions, and reciprocate your good wishes. Ladies and gentlemen, once again we thank you from the very bottom of our hearts!

63. THE LADIES

Generally Proposed by the Youngest Bachelor Present

Gentlemen,—

It is my duty as the only Bachelor here to-night to propose the health of the Ladies. It is a task which is usually accepted with avidity, and it is only when one rises to one's feet and looks into the faces one is addressing that its difficulties are realized.

Of course, the faces of the men don't matter; they can be divided, metaphorically of course, into two classes: those who feel certain they could do the job much better, and those who thank their lucky stars they have not to do it at all.

But upon the fair faces of the ladies present there sits an almost painful passivity and imperturbability; they know full well that the speaker dare say no word against them. No matter how he has suffered from their whims or from that member which is especially unruly when possessed by women, the speaker still must perform his task. Should he show ignorance he is dubbed a booby, should he show knowledge he is labelled a Lothario. You may think it extraordinary, my fair listeners, that we do not ask you all to our meetings. I can, however, assure you that it is not because we do not desire your company, but because the intolerable dullness of our usual proceedings would so weary you of our society that we should not then be able to look forward to your presence on our Annual Ladies' Nights.

It is at these male orgies that we look forward to basking in that all too unaccustomed blaze of culture and refinement which we gain by your presence here to-night. We are no worse than other men, but we are pretty bad—and we feel that sometimes at least we must recivilize ourselves: this can only be done by the softening influence which the presence of women affords.

I believe that in honouring the toast of our Lady Guests

to-night we are really pledging ourselves to civilization and undertaking to cast away the more uncouth practices of barbarism which are so dear to many of us.

Civilization, thy name is Woman, for without her where are our milliners' shops, our ball-rooms, or even our great tobacco industry? Let me finish by quoting from one of our greatest poets—

> "When Eve brought woe to all mankind
> Old Adam called her woe-man,
> But when she'd woo'd with love so kind
> He then pronounced her woman.
> But now, with folly and with pride,
> Their husbands' pockets trimming,
> The ladies are so full of whims
> The people call them w(h)imen."

Gentlemen, I bid you rise and drink the health of the Ladies.

64. THE LADIES

Proposed by a Guest

Mr. Chairman and Gentlemen,—

Let me say at once that I am too youthful, too unskilled in the study of the enchanting ways of womanhood to do justice to what is, no doubt, a great and inspiring subject. It is a theme on which I am lamentably ignorant, although not quite without interest, for I once replied "Where indeed!" to the profound thinker who startled me with the query, "Where would the world be without women?"

Gentlemen and Ladies, one thing has always struck me as strange—that it is to a bachelor that this toast of "The Ladies" is generally entrusted. Surely that is wrong, surely some married man who knows more than I can do of the charming sex should propose a toast such as this, and not one who has never met the lady of whom he could say—

> "Thou art my life, my love, my heart,
> The very eyes of me,
> And hast command of every part
> To love and die for thee."

The bachelor's knowledge is confined to researches in such works as the *Encyclopædia Britannica*, and from arduous study I can only conclude that nature has endowed the fair sex with all their many charms and graces for the purpose of making them fit partners for the god-like being whom they marry.

I wonder why no married man ever proposes this toast. Perhaps it is that none can find words eloquent enough. On the other hand, perhaps—again I wonder.

Gentlemen, I would in all seriousness say that any man who has achieved some success will tell you, and justly too, that he owes much, if not all of it, to the mother who watched with tender care over his youth, and to the wife in whom he ever found consolation and repose after the stress of the fight, and encouragement to strive anew. But there is nothing that I can say in praise of the ladies which is not already well-grounded in the heart of each one of you. So I call upon you to drink heartily to the Ladies, in due appreciation of the blessings we possess in our sweethearts and wives. Gentlemen, the Ladies.

65. REPLY TO THE TOAST OF THE LADIES

Mr. Chairman, Ladies and Gentlemen,—

My difficulty in replying to this toast is that women are supposed by tradition to be not only weaker but more modest than men. We are such shy, retiring creatures. When we are paid nice compliments, we are expected to do nothing but blush and look pretty, and you men have invented a large variety of cosmetics to assist us in both these occupations.

Not only are we forbidden from replying, but we are not allowed to retort, either. If one of us dares to step forward and say what she thinks about men in general, her reputation is gone for ever—whatever it is that she says. If her remarks are complimentary, she is put down as brazen and forward—hussy, I think the word is; if, on the other hand, she is uncomplimentary, she is—well, I understand that the Greeks had a word for it, and I can think of an English one, but if I used it I don't know what you would think of me!

The one bright spot from my point of view is that I have said such shocking things in my time that I must have lost my reputation long ago, so that it really does not seem to matter what I say now. So I will tell you frankly that I think men are wonderful—especially the ones who know how to flatter a woman!

That remark was on behalf of myself, although I'm sure I

would find plenty of supporters. On behalf of all the ladies, however, I am very happy to express my sincere thanks for the cordial way in which you have received this toast.

66. ANOTHER REPLY

Mr. Chairman, Gentlemen,—

On behalf of the other ladies present and on my own behalf, I thank you very heartily for the way this toast has been proposed and honoured. The great advantage about replying to a toast, from a woman's point of view, is that it satisfies her traditional love of having the last word. We are not averse from having the first word, either. Two neighbours were discussing a young married couple who had come to live near them. Said neighbour Number One, "The Smythes are an ideal couple—they think alike about everything." Neighbour Number Two replied, "Yes, but I notice *she* usually thinks it first." Well, that is the way of our sex; we think quickly, so we want the first word, and because we are always right—I defy you ever to force from a woman an admission that she is wrong—we must have the last word.

I am particularly grateful to the proposer for not contrasting the brightness and cleverness of women to-day with the insipidity of Victorian women. That always annoys me, because it is untrue. Women have always been bright and clever, but they were not always allowed to show it. Those Victorian women were our equals in most things, in some our superiors. If women now for the first time were asserting themselves one would deem it a mere flash in the pan. No, we women are as we always were: it is you who have changed. We are not cleverer than our ancestors: you *are* more generous than yours; you encourage manifestations of feminine equality where they denied or sneered at them. Again I thank you all.

67. THE GUESTS

Proposed by the Vice-Chairman

Mr. Chairman and Gentlemen,—

Before we separate I would ask you to join with me in drinking the health of our Guests. It has been a great pleasure to have them with us, and we owe them this meed of thanks for the compliment they have paid us by their presence, and for the geniality and good feeling they have diffused. Many of the Guests are already old friends, and all the others, we hope, will become so. [Some graceful allusion should be made to the more prominent of the Guests, particularly, of course, to the responder.] I know you will cordially drink with me the toast of their good health.

68. REPLY TO THE TOAST OF THE GUESTS
By One of Them

Mr. Chairman, Mr. Vice-Chairman and Gentlemen,—

You have entertained us royally, you have lavished kindness and hospitality on us, and just when we are wondering how to thank you, you take the breath out of our mouths by thanking us. Why you should do so, we cannot guess, but as we cannot be so rude as to contradict our hosts we must believe that in some way hidden from us we have conferred a favour upon you by having a good time as your charges. Well, I can only say that I shall be happy to confer the favour again, and as often as you like. In all sincerity we are very much obliged to you for honouring this toast so warmly and for the generous hospitality of which it marks the close. If the test of a good host is the enjoyment of his guests, you may claim that title, for we one and all have enjoyed ourselves. In the name of the Guests I thank you very much, and congratulate you upon the success of the function at which we have been honoured by being allowed to assist.

69. FAREWELL AND PRESENTATION TO A FRIEND
At a Dinner

Gentlemen,—

The occasion of our meeting here to-night is both a sad and a happy one—sad because we are met to say farewell to an old friend, happy because he is going away to take up a better position. It is, therefore, with very mixed feelings that I rise to give you the toast of "Our Guest" and to wish him, on your behalf as on my own, every success in his new life; we are very glad, indeed, that he is going to a position where his energy and abilities will have fuller scope, even while we are sorry to lose him from amongst us.

Gentlemen, I am not going to sing his praises—that would be at once impertinent and unnecessary—I shall only say that during his stay here our friend has endeared himself to us all by his never-failing kindness, hospitality, and consideration, as well as by his constant cheerfulness, good-fellowship and sympathy, qualities which will make him friends wherever he goes.

Though he will be no longer with us, I am sure that neither he nor we will soon forget our friendship, the pleasant comradeship and intimacy of many years. These things will be treasured memories to us all, and it is not in any fear that he will forget that we ask him to accept as a parting gift from us this [——] in token of our great regard and esteem. If gifts are valuable according to the feelings of the givers, then this one, in itself trifling, will perhaps commend itself more to him than other more precious objects solely because it is the gift of friends.

Now, gentlemen, I shall add no more than this—wherever he goes he takes with him our goodwill and our friendship, whenever he returns he will find us ready to welcome him. Raise your glasses and drink "Long Life, Good Luck and Prosperity to ——."

70. REPLY TO THE FOREGOING TOAST

Old Friends,—

I have no words in which to express my thanks to you, not only for the kind things that have been said about me, but also for this magnificent gift, which will always be amongst my most treasured possessions.

It was not without much very careful consideration that I made up my mind to leave a place where I have been so happy and have made so many real friends, but, gentlemen, Opportunity comes but seldom, and if you do not grasp her when she comes, she may never return, and I felt that I owed it to my wife and family not to let this chance slip. Need I say how sad I am to lose so many good and true friends, how much it costs me to go from you to strangers?—it is like leaving a part of myself behind. If my life here has been a happy one—and it has—it is to you, to your friendship and your company, that I owe it all. Be assured that I shall never forget you, and remember that, wherever it is, you are always welcome to my home; nothing could hurt me more than to know that any of you should be within reach and fail to visit me.

For your good wishes, too, I thank you from the bottom of my heart; in return will you accept my own? May you prosper and be happy as you deserve. I can say no more but this,—Again and again I thank you.

71. ON THE OCCASION OF A DINNER IN HONOUR OF A FRIEND AFTER LONG ABSENCE ABROAD

Gentlemen,—

The circumstances which have brought us together to-night afford us a golden opportunity of spending a pleasant and truly jolly evening. These dinners are always delightful functions, but to-night our pleasure is twofold—not only do we see the faces of our friends and neighbours, but we have amongst us Mr. ——, our guest, who not so many years ago occupied such a prominent and responsible position in our midst and whose close and enduring friendship to many of us meant so much in our daily lives. No longer perhaps are we entitled to refer to him as a neighbour, nevertheless we claim him, and with good reason, as one of our oldest and most trusted friends. Those of us who had the privilege of knowing him while he lived here have never forgotten his many acts of kindness to all sorts and conditions of people, his unfailing charm of manner, his cheerful disposition, and above all, his unfailing support of every movement which was for the benefit of the neighbourhood. Time cannot erase these things from our memories, and we are proud to think that our friend has not forgotten old times in the heyday of success. Gentlemen, let me tell you that one of his first thoughts on his return to the old country was to seek an opporunity of visiting the scenes of his earlier days. The ties of neighbourliness are often material, but the bonds of friendship are made of more lasting stuff, which neither time nor space can destroy. So, gentlemen, although our friend has been separated from us for a long time we somehow feel to-night that he has always been present with us.

Gentlemen, in bidding him welcome back to his old home—I am sure he feels that he is at home—I would remind you that he left at the call of duty—duty to his family and to himself. With all our hearts we congratulate him on his brilliant success, so honestly sought, and so well deserved.

Gentlemen, fill your glasses and drink the health of our guest, and bid him—"Welcome home."

72. REPLY TO THE FOREGOING TOAST

Gentlemen,—

I am so overwhelmed with the warmth of your reception, that I am wholly at a loss to find adequate words to express my thanks to you. I must ask you, therefore, to excuse my shortcomings in this respect, and to believe me when I say how deeply grateful I am, not only for the kind things which have been said about me on this occasion, but for all the good things which you have done to me in the past.

Gentlemen, although it is idle for me to deny that my life abroad has been happy and successful, I can honestly say that I was looking forward more than words can tell to a visit to the old home, and to this reunion with my old friends. Success I have had—perhaps more than I deserve—but I feel I can truly say that I never envied the success of anybody else.

Gentlemen, I will only repeat that I am glad to be with you once more, and again thank you from the bottom of my heart.

73. ABSENT FRIENDS

Proposed at a Dinner

Ladies and Gentlemen,—

The toast I am about to propose is one that, even on the most festive occasions, provokes a touch of sadness, yet it is one which we would not willingly let pass unhonoured. I give you "Absent Friends." It means much to us, this simple toast. Some of us have left home, family and friends in the old country to find a new home and new friends here, and on occasions such as this our thoughts must for a moment turn across the waters to those dear ones who are far away. Others will think of those of their family who have gone to other lands in pursuit of fame or fortune; hardly one of us but has kith or kin far away to whom his thoughts will turn as he lifts his glass to drink this toast. All of us have friends whom we miss, scattered in the far parts of the earth, severed from us by miles of land and leagues of ocean, but with us, we believe, in spirit. In silence let us drink to them—"Absent Friends!"

74. AT THE ANNUAL DINNER OF A LITERARY SOCIETY

Proposal of a Vote of Thanks to a Distinguished Chairman

Gentlemen,—

I rise to propose a vote of thanks to our Chairman, and I regret that the lateness of the hour compels me to be brief. Already some of you are looking at your watches and making calculations relative to the speed of taxis and the catching of last trains. I could say a good deal about our Chairman. He is, as you know, a prominent publicist, an admired writer and a pillar of British finance. That such a man should give up a whole evening to us is a compliment that we appreciate. Our proceedings have taken on a new dignity from his presence, and our speakers have surpassed themselves owing to the keen and appreciative hearing that he, a past-master in after-dinner oratory, has given them. It must have been an inspiration to address him.

A poor widow was mourning the recent death of a husband. "Such a husband as he was. Husband! he was more like a friend than a husband." Recalling this banquet we shall be able to say, "Such a Chairman —— —— was. Chairman!— he was more like a friend than a Chairman." Gentlemen, I ask you to drink the health of our Chairman —— ——.

75. REPLY TO THE FOREGOING TOAST

I thank you, gentlemen, for drinking the toast of my health so cordially, and you, Mr. ——, for eulogizing me so mistakenly—for praise is pleasant, even when undeserved. Your reference to me as a master of after-dinner oratory made me glad that the lateness of the hour forbade my being asked to give a sample of my alleged powers. You were within the mark, however, in saying that I listened with close attention to the speeches that have been delivered to-night. I did, and enjoyed every one of them. I love good speaking, and so do you all, although my young friends, probably, keep in the fashion by professing to be utterly bored by oratory of every kind. Despite the hoary antiquity of cave drawings, persuasive speech is the oldest of the arts. As compared with music, which competed with it to-night for your favour, oratory is the more distinctively human. A nightingale, unless it be a broadcasting bird, outsings any prima donna, who is delighted if told that she sings like a nightingale, whereas it is a left-handed compliment to declare that an orator talks like a parrot. I have enjoyed your hospitality, and I am glad to hear that you think my presence has contributed to the success of this most interesting gathering. Gentlemen, Mr. ——, I thank you.

76. MEETING OF A MASONIC LODGE

Proposing the Health of a Worshipful Master

Brethren,

To be chosen as your mouthpiece to wish health and continued prosperity to our Worshipful Master is to me a great honour—the highest that has fallen to me during my Masonic career.

To express concerning him the full meed of our admiration, respect, and affection, would sound, to one who did not know him, as an effort of fulsome flattery, and would be unnecessary; for we who are not strangers to him, and are conscious of the good influence of his life, are able to regard him as a Mason in the highest, noblest sense of the term; and what that implies we are all of us aware.

We see in this world so much of bitterness and rivalry, jealousy and bad feeling, that it is for mankind to be sure that in this our great and mystic Brotherhood a system exists which creates and encourages kindly sympathy, cordial and widespread benevolence and brotherly love; for the true Mason thinks no evil of his brother, and can cherish no evil design against him.

Further, I may say, and to this you can all bear witness, that Masonry is a religious system. In the Masonic Lodge the Bible is never closed and prayer is habitually used. If the whole human race could be guided by the principles of Masonry, for ever would be banished those selfish and hard feelings which divide and distract society, and fill the world with unrest. To say that the Brotherhood of Man is the principle of Masonry is not to proclaim from the housetops any secret of that widespread Society. Its principles were proclaimed in King Solomon's time, and found their perfect expression in the Sermon on the Mount; its Sacred Light shines in every Lodge throughout the world.

Gentlemen—Brothers—it is my proud duty, my pleasure, to give you the toast of the health of our greatly honoured Worshipful Master. May his light and influence long remain to guide and help us.

77. A SMOKING CONCERT

Opening Remarks by the Chairman

Gentlemen,—

Much to my satisfaction, and no doubt to yours also, a formal speech will not be required of me this evening. Although silence may be golden on an occasion such as the present, yet I would not be doing my duty as a Chairman if I did not say a word or two of the pleasure of the Committee, and especially the promoters and managers of the Concert, at your presence here this evening. In their name I bid you welcome and hope you will enjoy the items indicated in our programme; and I am sure it is right to relieve the strain and stress of the bustle and worry of our life by relaxation and an occasional "night off"; and he was a wise rhymester who penned the lines,—

> "A little nonsense now and then,
> Is relished by the wisest men."

I was reading the other day of two civic dignitaries, the retiring Lord Mayor and his successor, who were present, in 1800, at the usual festivities at the Mansion House. The outgoing Lord Mayor was known as a lover of his pipe and one was, accordingly, placed on the table before him. The incoming Lord Mayor had the good nature to share in the humour of his predecessor, and they were observed, after dinner, lighting their pipes (long clay ones known as churchwardens) at one candle, like the two Kings of Brentford in the old play, who placed their two old heads together and solemnly smelt at one nosegay.

Some gentlemen are already filling their pipes. Let me follow their good example. I will now call upon —— to open the programme.

78. AT THE END OF THE PROGRAMME

The Chairman Again

Gentlemen,—

The best of friends must part and so must we. But before we sing a verse or two of "Auld Lang Syne," it is my pleasure and privilege to offer our warmest thanks to those who have contributed so generously to our amusement to-night. You have, indeed, at various stages of our programme shown your appreciation of their services, but you would, I am sure, wish me to emphasize your applause, expressing to the different artists your sincere gratitude. I daresay that they, on their part, are fully aware of the support you have given them by your presence as well as your approval, for a "full house" makes the rendering of a song or other number considerably easier. I have never been able to forget *Punch's* picture of the comic man struggling with an unsympathetic audience, and I do really believe, therefore, that our artist friends to-night probably thank you almost as cordially as you thank them. [Add here if necessary: Gentlemen, I have the greatest pleasure in proposing a hearty vote of thanks to the artists.]

CHAPTER XVII

SPORTING TOASTS

79. AT A CRICKET DINNER—"OUR OPPONENTS"

Proposed by the Captain of the Victorious Eleven

Gentlemen,—

As Chairman of this very pleasant gathering, I have a toast to propose to you which, after what has already passed to-day, and judging by the good feeling apparent among us, I am sure the team of which I have the honour to be captain will drink with much pleasure. The toast is the health of the —— Eleven, our courteous and able opponents in the field. We have had an excellent game, and though by the glorious uncertainties of cricket it has so happened that our team won the match, we are quite ready to acknowledge what trouble we had to make the runs, and to avoid the ready hands in the field, and keep up our stumps, before bowling such as our friends can command. I am glad for the honour of our club that we won, though I am sure—if my friend the captain of your team will permit me to say so—that if close fielding and steady work deserve success (as they do) we shall not win again in a hurry nor easily. Now, gentlemen, I need not detain you much longer.

Winners and losers alike, we have had a good game and enjoyed it, and I trust we may have many others. Gentlemen, I give you the —— Eleven, coupled with the name of Mr. ——, that most able captain and cricketer, and my very good friend.

80. RESPONSE TO THE FOREGOING TOAST

By the Captain of the Opposing Team

Mr. Chairman, Mr. Vice-Chairman, and Gentlemen,—

Your Captain has proposed our health in such very complimentary terms, and expressed himself so kindly towards his beaten but not humiliated adversaries, that I cannot quite decide in my own mind which to admire most—his prowess with the bat and in the field or his courtesy and eloquence

153

off it. At any rate I need not try to decide now. I have to thank him for the manner in which the toast was proposed, and you, gentlemen, for the way in which it has been honoured. You won a well-contested match, and we have no excuses to make for our defeat; we can only say that the better team won. But we are not going to sit down and accept this issue as final. We do not intend—and I think my friends will agree with me that we are right—we do not mean to give in. We hope you will meet us again, and on our own ground, where if we cannot entertain you as hospitably and as generously as we have been entertained here—though we will try that too—we will certainly be delighted to meet you and do our very best to beat you handsomely. From our games I think we get not only pleasure but considerable profit—for it is always a good thing to keep fit—and when the time comes when the pavilion and not the playing field is our place, we shall remember with pleasure many a hard-fought game and, no doubt, tell a younger generation how play has gone off since "our time." Gentlemen of the —— Cricket Club, I will only add my thanks and those of my colleagues for the very kind reception you have given us.

A CRICKET CLUB ANNUAL DINNER

81. SUCCESS TO THE —— CLUB

Proposed by the Chairman

Gentlemen,—

You are doubtless anticipating the usual speech from the chair, and I will not keep you in suspense very long nor tire your patience. The report of the club, showing its financial position and the result of the last season's working, has already been placed before you. You will have noticed that the matches in which the club [and ground] engaged were more numerous last season than in the previous years. The receipts from members, and subscriptions, have increased, and there are two very satisfactory points connected with the past season, viz., the funds are in good condition, we having a very respectable balance in hand, and the club has won [nine], lost [four], and drawn [three] of the matches it has played against other elevens.

I am glad to welcome so many new members to our ranks;

but the number must necessarily be limited. We have not accommodation for more than a certain number, and on one or two occasions already some dissatisfaction has been expressed at the want of accommodation. Well, gentlemen, the committee have done all they can, and have succeeded in keeping the club solvent. But if more accommodation for match days is to be provided—and the committee were glad to see that ladies mustered in larger numbers to encourage them—they would suggest a slightly increased entrance fee upon big match days, or the issue of season tickets to friends of the members duly introduced. This would give them a fund to draw upon and entitle the holders to seats.

There have been no accidents of any consequence, and some excellent cricket has been shown. We have now a very excellent eleven, and I am happy to be able to announce that there are some promising "colts" in the district, who will have an opportunity of trying their mettle on an early day in the ensuing season.

I am glad to see that our national game still keeps its hold upon the country. I do not think cricket was ever more popular. We have seen teams from both hemispheres giving a good account of themselves, showing great patience when an up-hill game had to be played, and by brilliant dash and rapid scoring eventually pulling a game "out of the fire." What man has done man may do, and I hope the day is far distant when matches between England and her children will cease to be played. Especially must we learn to take defeat in as sportsmanlike a spirit as victory, for both are equal tests of character, and to rejoice that our kindred beyond sea have such a relish for the old England sport, and prove so readily that they are real chips of the old block, possessing all the good qualities of the race of Englishmen. There is a good deal to be said about the game, but as so many of you here are much more familiar with the practice than I am, I will spare you my theories as to the mode of playing it; and my moral reflections I am sure you will be content to take, like the report, as read. Gentlemen, I have now only to give you the toast I rose so long ago to propose, and for which you have so kindly waited. I will try your patience no longer. Success to the —— Cricket Club, and I will couple with the toast the name of the Hon. Secretary, Mr. ——, to whose exertions the club owes so much of its success.

82. RESPONSE TO THE FOREGOING TOAST

By the Hon. Secretary of the Club

Mr. Chairman, Mr. Vice-Chairman, and Gentlemen,—

It is very gratifying to me to hear my name coupled with the success of the —— Cricket Club, and the feeling ought to be—but, alas! for poor human nature, is not—diminished by the reflection that the honour is in great part undeserved. The Committee, of which I am only a member and the mouthpiece, has really done all the work, but what I have done I can assure you I have done very willingly. I am very fond of the game, and at one time took some little part in it. Should circumstances and occupations permit, I may again be able to put aside the pen for the ball, and sing, "Oh, willow, willow," when I grasp my old bat once more, and go in to score yet another "duck." I am very glad that the club is in such a flourishing condition, in the ledgers as well as in the scoring books, and I heartily endorse the proposal, put forward by our Chairman, that we should increase the accommodation for match days. Rather than increase the entrance fee I would advocate the issue of season tickets to a limited number of the friends of members. The matches have been won by sheer hard work and careful coaching, and for this increasing success the club is mainly indebted to Mr. ——, our energetic captain. The success is his, and his men have *backed him up* well. He has been bold as a bowler, and his manner of *driving* shows how well he is fitted to handle a *team*. We all have recognized his *powers of defence*, and have never known him *stumped* in argument or repartee. With such qualities he appears *cut* out for the position of captain, and I hope that the time is *long off* when he will retire. That he will make a *point* of *long stopping* with us, and leading the eleven to victory, for many more seasons, is, I am sure, our heartfelt wish. Gentlemen, in thanking you for the honour you have done me, I would crave permission to propose the health of Mr. ——, the Captain of the Eleven.

83. RESPONSE OF THE CAPTAIN TO THE FORE-GOING TOAST

Mr. Chairman and Gentlemen,—

My friend the Honorary and honourable Secretary has made a speech so bristling with cricket terms as to be almost *wicked!* and I feel in danger of following his example in that sense—but I forbear. I am quite unable to meet him on that ground; he may claim to score off me there. But I am none the less grateful to him, gentlemen, for the very clever and pleasant manner in which the last toast was proposed and to you for the way in which it was received. "The labour we delight in physics pain," and I really cannot lay claim to all the good qualities which my friend attributes to me, for I am so fond of cricket, and I may add of the club, that any inconvenience or trouble falls from me when the necessities or the demands of the game or the club make themselves known, or are made known, as they generally are, to me by my friend your un-wearying secretary. The eleven last season was a very good one, and I must in mere fairness remark that if our men had not displayed pluck and determination, if they had not worked so well together, my labours as captain would have been im-mensely increased. It is always a grateful theme with me, and when we have such men in the eleven as —— and ——, there need be no misgivings when we take the field; and no fear of bad seasons, with ordinary luck, while we possess such bowlers as —— and such sure fieldsmen as —— and ——. It is an honour to captain such a team, and I feel it so, I assure you. Gentlemen, I thank you heartily for your good wishes, and for the kindness with which you have listened to my imperfect oratory.

AN ASSOCIATION FOOTBALL CLUB DINNER

84. THE —— CLUB

Proposed by the Chairman

Gentlemen,—

It has been suggested that I should say a few words about the history of Association Football for the benefit of young players, but it would occupy more than the few minutes allotted to me to give even a condensed history of our great game. I can, however, briefly indicate three important stages in its development.

First, the introduction of the off-side rule, an innovation that transformed the game, changing it almost beyond recognition, as all will allow who remember how in the past it was the custom for an opposing player to wait upon the sorely-tried goal-keeper and charge him without mercy when the forwards bombarded the goal. Secondly, the introduction of Cup Ties came as an inspiration, and increased tenfold the interest of the public in the "Soccer" game; while the creation of League Football proved of intense importance in captivating the minds of enthusiasts right away from the beginning of the season to the end.

Objection is often raised by purists to the system known as the purchase of players, by professional clubs, by which a weak team is strengthened through the inclusion of new blood brought in from across the Border or elsewhere; and certainly this trade of buying and selling seems a blot on the scutcheon of a great game. To see a number of ruddy-haired players issue from the dressing quarters of an English club, and hear them revealing their ancestry in a dialect made immortal by association with Bobbie Burns and Walter Scott, gives one cause for wonder whether we are indeed out to watch an English League game. But even in this direction matters are not so bad as they were; and, after all, these players from Scotland delight us with their knowledge of the game and their great skill. They have undoubtedly improved English Football by the introduction of their methods and ideas, and most of the leading English players have been quick to seize upon the points that matter and incorporate them in their own game, and we who love the splendid game know that English Association has been improved by the recognition of the Scottish element in our English clubs. Association Football is a great and noble game, and we welcome all who try to improve it, whether they come from the far north or hail from counties further south. When I rose to-night I mentioned our young players. We have in the club quite a number of youngsters of promise and they are all exceptionally keen. This augurs well for the club, and I am confident that we need have no fears for its prosperity in the future.

Gentlemen, I will conclude by asking you to drink with me to the continued prosperity of the —— Football Club.

A RUGBY FOOTBALL CLUB DINNER

85. THE —— CLUB

Proposed by the Chairman

For many years it has been the custom of the Chairman of our Club on this occasion of our Annual Dinner to propose the toast of the —— Club, and to deliver himself eloquently—or, as in my own case, otherwise—on matters of special interest to Rugby Football. So much has been said on the subject that, as this evening approached, I began to fear that I should be "gravelled for lack of matter." Then, luckily for me, a schoolboy came to my rescue—or rather the ghost of one, for the boy would have lived close upon a century and a half had he survived to this day.

It was in 1823 that William Webb Ellis, a Rugby schoolboy, while taking part in a game, caught the ball, and so far from observing the practice of that time, of retiring back and either kicking it himself, or placing it for someone else to kick, rushed forward with the ball in his hands towards the opposite goal. This action of Ellis struck the fancy of his own and other schools, and became, after a few years, so generally followed, that, about 1840, it was officially recognized as a legitimate part of the game, and became so generally accepted by Rugby men that, on the wall overlooking the School playing-fields, a tablet was placed with an inscription, of which I have a copy— "This stone commemorates the exploit of William Webb Ellis, who, with a fine disregard for the rules of football, as played in his time, first took the ball in his hands and ran with it, thus originating the distinctive feature of the Rugby Game, A.D. 1823."

The incident seems to have set players thinking of possible developments of the game, and may no doubt be accepted as marking the start of the distinctive feature in Rugby Football.

From a crude and no doubt rather brutal pastime in its earliest stages, the game has so developed that to-day it supplies not only a vigorous and healthy exercise but also a splendid discipline. It calls for strength and pace, quickness of eye, hand and foot, intelligence to seize an opportunity in attack, and pluck and resource in times of pressure. While by some old folks it may still be regarded as nothing more than an outlet for the native savagery of the race, to those of us who have played the game it has become something of a religion. We know its good effects upon the youth of the race, and we realize that so long as it is played in the proper spirit its possibilities for good are far-reaching.

We are proud of the game and we love it, and I know you will readily respond to the toast of continued prosperity to the —— Football Club, especially as I couple with the toast the name of Mr. ——, our Hon. Secretary, who has done so much for our success.

A GOLF CLUB DINNER

86. CONTINUED PROSPERITY OF OUR CLUB

Proposed by the Chairman

Gentlemen,—

It is always easy to propose the welfare and success of ourselves, for, practically, that is what such a toast as this comes to. But in this case it is a pleasure also, for everyone who plays the Royal and Ancient game of Golf knows that to it he—and I am happy to think I must also say she—owes perfect relaxation from the cares of life and the worries of the household, as well as the increased enjoyment of health and strength, and this, whether he has a *plus* handicap or still remains amongst the unhandicapped. For golf is not only a game of skill but a life-giving pastime. The exercise it affords is in no sense violent, but it is complete. The revival of the game is one of the extraordinary facts in the history of Sport. Golf links in England in the mid-Victorian period might almost have been counted on the fingers; to-day they are found everywhere. One of the greatest advantages of golf is that it can be played at any season of the year. There is no need to fix up your team some time ahead, as in the case of cricket or football. Somebody willing and eager to "have a round" will nearly always be found waiting at the club.

Our club has shared in the general prosperity of the game, and we will do our best to maintain and even increase its well-being.

I will couple the toast of Prosperity to our Club that I have now the pleasure to propose with the name of our deservedly popular Secretary, the genial Mr. ——.

87. REPLY TO THE FOREGOING TOAST

By the Secretary of the Club

Mr. Chairman,—

You have spoken of our game in terms that all golfers will accept without question, but the scoffer, perhaps, would remind you that you said nothing about the language with which it is supposed to be decorated, or, rather, with which players are occasionally tempted to adorn their strokes. Even the cloth cannot always resist this temptation, as witness the story of the reverend gentleman who, whenever he foozled a stroke, was wont to exclaim angrily "Sennar!" explaining to any who inquired why he did so, that it was "the biggest dam on earth." Yet despite this, and after making every deduction, even the scoffer cannot deny that golf is one of the grandest outdoor games ever invented. And, moreover, it does teach some moral discipline. Look at its familiar maxims—"far and sure," "keep your eye on the ball," "don't press," and the like. Have they no bearing on everyday life? Do they not teach us to "keep a straight line" in life as on the course? Consider, too, the lessons to be learned in a bunker: is there anything more calculated to teach patience and perseverance than a series of well-placed bunkers.

As to the immediate subject of the toast, I think my fellow-members need have no anxiety. Our club is going along very comfortably, we have a competent and obliging professional, who keeps the course in good order, and we have the real club spirit among our members; these should be sufficient to ensure its continued prosperity. In the name of the club, I thank you all for the very hearty way in which you have received this toast.

A MOTOR CLUB

88. THE —— MOTOR CLUB

Proposed by the President at the Annual Dinner

Gentlemen,—

The toast of the —— Motor Club which I now rise to propose is certain to receive a hearty response from you, however inadequate my words in proposing it may be. Motoring has long ceased to be the pastime of a few privileged ones. Indeed, congestion on the roads is our problem to-day; but I know that none of us would like to see any section of the motoring public deprived of its pleasure. The solution to the problem lies not in fewer motorists, but in more and better roads. The motoring trade has developed into a great industry, giving employment to many thousands of hands throughout the world. The man or woman who does not motor is now rather the exception, not the rule, and the all-conquering motor-car has crossed the Sahara and the arid wastes of Australia; in fact, there seems to be no limit to the capabilities and utility of the motor-car.

Clubs such as ours afford opportunities of pleasant social intercourse, and the periodical club run or hill-climb serves to take us into the fresh air and to present the opportunity for a most useful exchange of ideas to all who are wise enough to take part in them. I venture to say that there are many places of interest within a radius of one hundred miles from this room which many of us would never have visited but for the club pilgrimages. It is a theme upon which I should like to dilate, but even if I were more competent to do so than I am, it would be unnecessary to an audience who, I am sure, regard it with as much enthusiasm as I do. Gentlemen, I give you the toast, "Prosperity to the —— Motor Club."

AT A REGATTA DINNER

89. SUCCESS TO THE REGATTA

Proposed by the Chairman

Gentlemen,—

We have come to the toast of the day, and, as you will readily admit, it is an interesting one to all present. The occasion of the —— Regatta cannot possibly be dismissed in a few words. It is now an annual institution, and its success or failure means a good deal, not only to those immediately interested, but to all who are connected with the —— Club. I am glad to be able to chronicle a marked success to-day. We have seen some good and close racing; and if our crew did not carry off many laurels, they were, if defeated, certainly not disgraced, and we would rather see them win upon other water than their own. We prefer our visitors to carry off the prizes if they can. We are as pleased to see them win as to win ouselves, and the best men must win—of that we feel assured. We have done fairly well, but might have done better, and while condoling with the unsuccessful we can warmly congratulate the victors upon their success.

Let me now say a few words respecting the club and the business side of the question. The finances are in a pretty good condition, and even if I did not tell you, you could see from the beaming face of the Treasurer that we have a balance in hand, after providing for all expenses; it amounts to £——. [*Insert here any remarks as to future plans, finances, etc.*]

The general arrangements of the club have been much improved, and the success of the arrangements is in a great measure, if not altogether, due to the untiring efforts of Mr. ——, our most efficient honorary secretary. To him we all owe a deep debt of gratitude, and with his name I will conclude my remarks. I will call upon you all to drink to the health of Mr. ——, to whose tact and patience the prosperity and popularity of the club are in a great measure due. Gentlemen, raise your glasses, please, for the Honorary Secretary.

90. A REGATTA DINNER

Reply of the Hon. Secretary

Mr. Chairman and Gentlemen,—

I trust you will excuse me if, in my endeavours to thank you for your kind reception of the last toast, I fail to make myself as intelligible as I wish. The honour you have done me is unexpected, and all the more embarrassing to me on that account. It is very generous of our Chairman to speak of me in such terms. Though I have endeavoured to do my duty I have never done more; and therefore, conscientiously speaking, I have no claim to your thanks. But it is very gratifying, nevertheless, to feel and to hear that in the estimation of one's friends, and in the opinion of the Chairman, one has succeeded in one's endeavours. The Club House has been a very pleasant rendezvous, but not all the efforts of the Committee and Secretary would have accomplished everything without the hearty co-operation of the members. The Committee have been indefatigable and untiring in their efforts to make the club and its arrangements successful; and we think we have in a measure succeeded. Gentlemen, I thank you all very sincerely for the way you have drunk my health.

91. THE HEALTH OF THE COMPETING CREWS

Proposed by the Chairman

Gentlemen,—

I am going to propose a double toast, and one which you will, I know, be glad to honour. I mean the health of the two competing crews in the chief race. We were much interested to-day in the races for the Grand Challenge Cup, the final issue of which, as you are aware, was limited to the two boats whose crews are here present. We were beaten, and—well, not badly beaten. We accept with resignation our defeat, but we intend as soon as possible to reverse the verdict, if possible, and claim the Cup. There will be opportunities for us to retrieve our laurels soon, and we intend to try and regain some of them at any rate. Meanwhile I call upon you to drink first to our guests, the —— Crew, who have so well and honourably defeated us; and secondly, I will ask you to keep a little cheer for our own Eight, who struggled so gamely to pick up the race. Gentlemen, though they are opponents in these contests, I couple in all friendship and with all good wishes the toasts of the —— Crew and the Eight of the —— Club.

92. REPLY TO THE FOREGOING TOAST

By the Stroke of the Successful Boat

Mr. Chairman and Gentlemen,—

It is with some diffidence that I rise to reply to the toast which you, sir, have so handsomely proposed, and to which all your members have so kindly responded. I can assure you we think we are very lucky in having carried off the prize; and if anything can add to our satisfaction in having wrested it from such a fine crew, it is the generous and sporting manner in which that perhaps temporary defeat has been taken and our success welcomed. Such kindness as we have met at your hands increases the value of the prize fourfold. We appreciate it all, I assure you, and although I cannot—and you will not expect me to—say I hope you will regain it, I am certain of one thing : that never was a losing race more pluckily rowed, and never was a defeat more admirably taken nor more courteously acknowledged.

We have had many pleasant meetings during the period in which I have been stroking the Eight of the —— Club, and it has fallen to my lot, I am glad to say, to have been partly the means of winning some prizes; but mainly on account of the gallant and sporting struggle of our opponents on the present occasion we value our prize to-day most highly.

We trust your excellent crew will pay us a visit at our regatta, and in the name of our club, the ——, I may say that you will be very welcome.

Gentlemen, once more in the name of the Eight of —— I thank you for the honour you have done us in drinking our healths.

CHAPTER XVIII
BUSINESS TOASTS

93. CHAIRMAN'S SPEECH
Annual General Meeting

Ladies and Gentlemen,—

Before proceeding to the formal business of our meeting, it is my melancholy duty to refer to the loss we have sustained since we last met through the death of Mr. X., one of our Directors. His whole-hearted devotion to the interests of the Company and the knowledge and skill he brought to bear on its problems won the admiration of his colleagues, just as his considerateness and geniality won our warm regard. His personal qualities were such that we feel we have lost a sincere friend, and we express our own sorrow and our deep sympathy with the members of his family.

You will see that the share capital has increased from £—— to £—— owing to the issue of —— shares last year. Loans from Bankers—secured by deposit of Debentures—which were £—— last year, have been reduced to £——. We are writing off £—— for depreciation. The profit for the fourteen months is £——, which is again a record for the company. The assets show freehold land and buildings, £——. The rolling stock has been increased by additions to £——. Plant, stock and furniture have all been rigorously written down to present-day values and there only remains the goodwill figure of £——.

The profit, after making provision for taxation and depreciation, Directors' fees and Managing Directors' remuneration, is £——. The dividend on the Preference shares for 19— takes £——, leaving £——. A dividend of 10 per cent. on the Ordinary shares will absorb £——, leaving a surplus of £——. Of this surplus it is proposed to carry to Reserve Account £——, and the balance of £—— is added to our carry-forward, making the total £——.

Given the absence of industrial trouble during the coming year, we may be able to reap more fully the fruits of the labour of the last few years, and also be able to devote still closer attention to increasing our sales and to the more economic handling of goods.

As we have branches in all the chief towns of the Kingdom, our business may fairly be represented as covering the whole country. The success of every branch has been well maintained, and it is with great pride that we pay a well-deserved tribute to the loyalty and business ability of our branch managers who worthily uphold the great traditions of our Company. It is hoped that in the ensuing year our representatives will visit Canada and Australia and other Commonwealth and foreign countries, and that these visits will lay the foundation of a successful export business.

As we look back on the past year our thanks are once again due to our Managing Directors for the able manner in which they have guided our affairs through a time of unprecedented difficulty. They have the loyal and able support of a most excellent staff, both at headquarters and in the branches, whom also we thank for their splendid contribution to the success of another year.

94. ELECTION OF A DIRECTOR OF A COMPANY

Proposed by the Chairman or Managing Director

Gentlemen,—

Always excepting my privilege as Managing Director of this important Company when I am able to declare a dividend high enough to be regarded as satisfactory by all concerned, there is nothing that gives me more pleasure than to be the mouthpiece for proposing that honour be conferred upon one of our members whose high character, sound business ability, and devotion to our service have very rightly won our wholehearted appreciation.

In moving that a Directorship in this Company be awarded to Mr. ——, for many years our most untiring and able Secretary, I must say that I feel, just for the moment, as if in the position of a monarch conferring a title upon some worthy citizen; only with this difference, that I am more intimately aware than any king could be in the case of a newly-made knight how deserving our Mr. —— is of the distinction the Company desire to bestow upon him.

From the day he became connected with the business he set himself to become master of every detail concerning it, and each stage of his advancement has been evidence of the efficiency he untiringly cultivated with such marked success.

My colleagues and I have the fullest confidence that it is in the best interests of the Company that he should fill the double rôle of Secretary and Director, and I feel sure that the proposition now put forward, that he be elected to a Directorship in the Company, will readily find a seconder.

95. RE-ELECTION OF DIRECTOR

Proposed by the Managing Director of a Company

Gentlemen,—

As you will have seen by the Report and Accounts already in your hands, the Company has good reason to feel happy about its ability to maintain its prosperity; at the same time it must be recognized that changes are in progress among other firms following an industry similar to ours, and that these changes are not altogether a good omen. For example, some important rival Companies are accepting foreign contracts at a figure that leaves a margin of profit perilously low if all goes as they hope, and no profit at all, but a thumping loss, should conditions prove adverse. I believe this is spoken of as a good progressive policy. So it is for the foreigners who benefit thereby. As your Directors, gentlemen, and the custodians of a valuable property, we have set our faces against such wild adventures. There is still guidance in the old adage—"Safety first."

Before passing on to a personal matter of great interest to myself, and I am sure to most who are present at this Annual Meeting, I will move the Adoption of the Report and Accounts, and the proposed payment of a dividend of —— per cent., less tax, on the Ordinary shares. I understand Mr. —— will second the motion. . . . For ——; Against, ——; Carried unanimously.

Now I turn to the subject of personal interest, which is to move the re-election of Mr. —— as a Director. He has for a number of years been in close personal association with me, and I have knowledge of his worth as a man and of his rare judgment as a business official. If I know bedrock necessities, practical impossibilities, and varied contingencies peculiar to the various sides of the business, I am sure Mr. —— knows them too. All the Directors are profoundly convinced that the co-operation of Mr. —— on the Directorate is most valuable and very desirable.

96. RESIGNATION OF A DIRECTOR

Regret Expressed by Chairman of Company

Gentlemen,—

Since the distribution of the printed Report to the Shareholders, Mr. —— has informed me, to my great regret, that owing to his election to the chairmanship of a great public body he will be compelled to resign most of his directorships, and among them that of our Company, so that he is unable to present himself for re-election.

I should like to take this opportunity of expressing on behalf of the shareholders, as well as of his fellow-Directors, our deep appreciation of the many services he has rendered to the Company during his long connection with it, and further to express the hope that, should it become possible in the future, we may welcome him once more to our Board.

97. VOTE OF THANKS TO MANAGING DIRECTOR AND STAFF

Proposed by the Chairman

Gentlemen,—

Before the meeting ends I should like to take the opportunity of expressing, on behalf of the Directors, our thanks for the loyal, useful, and devoted services which the whole staff, from the managing Director, the managers, and the Secretary downwards, have rendered during the past year. I am sure that such a vote will be appreciated, and I can say from my personal knowledge that it is no more than their due.

In the upper grades, and in the general staff, we have a team of men who are loyally devoted to the interests of the business. It is a great comfort to me in my responsibilities to know that I can rely upon such support, and I wish to express to them my personal thanks. By the earnest efforts of all they have succeeded in making the Company prosperous, and the success we have achieved is due to the combined endeavours of our staff from the heads of departments down to the most recently appointed juniors.

98. THE FIRM

Proposed by one of the Employees

Mr. Chairman, Mr. Vice-Chairman and Gentlemen,—

By an honour of which I am fully conscious it devolves upon me to propose to you the health of the Firm with which we all, or nearly all, are associated—I may say proudly associated. In the presence of our principals I will not dilate upon our many reasons for pride in their service—firstly because they themselves would object to my doing so, and secondly because such detail would be superfluous, as there is not one of us but can recall kindnesses and encouragements which have made working for these gentlemen a pleasure and the identification of our interests with theirs not merely easy but inevitable.

We can imagine what pleasure the Directors of a Firm feel when their business succeeds. When the manufacturer successfully launches a novelty on the sea of trade, or the merchant makes a *coup*, when the lawyer wins a case or the publisher introduces a "best seller," a Firm naturally rejoices in such an event; but it means much more when all the servants of the Firm rejoice as well. I have always liked Sir Walter Scott the better since I read the story of his gamekeeper who, when his master remarked that it was likely to be a good season for the crops, replied, "Yes, master! and I hope it will be a good season for our books."

I am certain that mutual regard and consideration between employers and employed are invaluable in the running of a great Firm such as this. No masters will be so well served as those who are both loved and respected, whose censure is just, whose criticisms, while not lacking at times in severity, are not sparing of praise where it is due.

Gentlemen, such employers are ours, and in that belief I call upon you all to drink health and prosperity to the Firm of Messrs. ——, and to thank them for the pleasant "outing" (or good dinner) to which they have invited us to-day.

99. REPLY TO THE FOREGOING TOAST

By the Senior Partner Present

Mr. Vice and Gentlemen,—

Being the Chairman I cannot address myself; but I have an indulgent Vice ready to listen to me, and perhaps to prompt me. We are—I speak also for my partners—we all are very sensible of the kindness with which the toast of our health has been proposed and received. It is true, as Mr. ——— said just now, that mutual consideration and esteem are invaluable between employers and employed, as indeed they are in all human relations; and we are delighted to hear from him that you all feel thus towards ourselves. Believe me the respect and regard are mutual. We have a staff to be proud of. Nothing pleased me more than a comment made by one of our visitors last year —"What a splendid body of men you have here!"

There is one point in the speech just delivered which I must touch upon—the importance of praising. I don't think Mr. ——— quite realized—or if he did his realization went unexpressed—the impossibility of there being any verbal recognition of every bit of work well done. We are willing and anxious to do all possible in this respect, but we can't spend the day patting worthy employees openly on the back; but this I will claim—that though much faithful work goes perforce unpraised none goes unrecognized. We are not blind, my partners and I, to what goes on, and each and all of you can rest assured of receiving credit where credit is due, even if no verbal bouquets are handed to you.

We are pleased that we can annually enjoy our holiday together as we have to-day. And now I will detain you no longer. There are many other toasts to come, I perceive, so I will at once resume my duties as Chairman after again thanking you for the toast which has been so ably proposed by Mr. ——— and received in a manner so highly gratifying to the Firm.

100. THE EMPLOYEES

Proposed by a Junior Director

Mr. Chairman, Mr. Vice-Chairman and Gentlemen,—

It is my pleasing duty to propose the health of the Employees of the Firm. In all large houses there must be a head and hands—just as in the human body we have a directing brain and limbs to obey the brain's directions. But unless the hands work with the head, unless the limbs respond quickly and willingly to the intellect, they are practically useless.

On the other hand, if the brain commands wrongfully, the man is vicious or even criminal; a curse to society and to himself. Perfection either in a man or in a machine implies clearness of head and capable, obedient members. This is the secret of success: honesty and ability in command, obedience and loyalty in service. These I maintain we have had, and to them we attribute the great advances our Firm has made.

We are glad to take this occasion to thank our staff not for their efficiency and loyalty alone, but also for their keenness, their constant concern for the Firm's good, for that extra bit of "snap," if I may use the word, that distinguishes the zealous worker from the merely competent. You, gentlemen, have shown that you have your hearts in your work, and we are grateful to you. In proposing the health of the Employees of the Firm, I couple with the toast the name of our valued servant and friend, Mr. ——.

101. REPLY TO THE TOAST OF THE EMPLOYEES

Mr. Chairman, Mr. Vice-Chairman, and Gentlemen,—

The employees have reason to thank you, Mr. ——, for the kind things you have said about us all, and the other Directors for their spontaneous and obviously sincere endorsement of them. In their name I do thank you all most heartily and also for your abounding hospitality to-day. Our annual dinners are anticipated early and looked back upon with extreme pleasure by us all, and to-day's, which I think is the most successful of the whole series, will certainly be no exception.

Touching the efforts of my colleagues, I believe they have all done their duty to the best of their abilities, willingly, conscientiously, and zealously. A great deal has been accomplished, and we are glad to know that the balance sheet shows that our efforts and yours, sirs, have not been unfruitful, and that the old House, for which many of us have worked so long and so pleasantly, continues to prosper. We trust that our efforts in the future will be at least as satisfactory, and that the mutual esteem and regard which influences all in the House will be even more firmly cemented.

Gentlemen, in the name of the employees I thank you for your goodwill.

102. FAREWELL AND PRESENTATION TO A BUSINESS COLLEAGUE UPON HIS RETIREMENT

Gentlemen,—

Our task this afternoon is at once pleasing and melancholy. We are saying farewell to a very old, a highly respected, let me add a deeply loved colleague, with whom some of us have worked for more than half a lifetime. The pleasant aspect of this gathering is that we are wishing our dear friend health and happiness and presenting him, in token of our esteem, with this grandfather clock. The appropriateness of the gift is not overwhelming, for with a man's retirement the importance of correct time-keeping departs. This morning to Mr. —— the catching of the 8.28 was all-important. To-morrow the 8.53 will serve equally well. But the selection was made by our friend after consultation with his family, and no doubt it will be appreciated. If gifts are valued according to the affection that prompted them, this grandfather clock will be a treasured possession indeed.

We are taking farewell of Mr. —— as a colleague. As that we shall never greet him again. But I expect he will often drop in upon us as a friend—or meet some of us at the old accustomed haunts for a cup of tea together or a game at dominoes, and whenever and wherever he meets one of us there will be a glad welcome. Old colleague, farewell. Dear old friend, we hope and expect to see you often.

103. ANOTHER SPEECH

[On these semi-informal occasions more than one may be asked to testify, so it is well to go prepared.]

Gentlemen,—

I don't know why, at the very last second, I am called upon, except as the successor of Mr. —— to the headship of the —— —— department. In case I should be called upon the staff under me asked me to say that Mr. —— has always been respected and loved in his department. I can endorse this, and if, when it comes to my turn to retire, I leave behind me as fragrant a memory, I shall be a proud man. Mr. —— would never ask anyone to do a thing he could not do himself. To this his success was due; he knew the work of his depart-

ment from top to bottom, and was in a position to see that
every one knew and *did* his job. Mr. ——, your old department wishes you all happiness.

104. REPLY TO THE FOREGOING

Mr. ——, Gentlemen,—

I thank you from my heart for the very kind things you have
said and thought about me. Yes, I have been encompassed
with kind wishes. I was conscious of them all the time Mr.
—— was speaking. And I am grateful for this very handsome
present, which *will* be valued in proportion to the kindness
behind the gift of it. And I thank Mr. —— for undertaking to
have it delivered at my door in one of the Firm's vans. You
were wondering how I could get it home, and if I should have
the experience of a man who, moving to a new home a hundred yards or so from the old, started out to carry his grandfather clock. The day was hot, the clock heavy, and he had to
set it down on the pavement to rest himself. An inquisitive
stranger addressed him : "Don't you think, sir, that in this hot
weather you would find a wrist-watch more convenient? It
would tell you the time equally well, and you would not have
to impede the traffic when you needed to consult it." It would,
and perhaps a wrist-watch would tell me the time as accurately
as this noble present of yours—that is, if I ever have need to
know the time, which Mr. —— doubts. But this grandfather
clock will tell me, as no other timepiece in the world could, of
good friends and well-wishers at —— and that it is time I
looked them up. Thank you again. In a few minutes I shall
walk out of this building for the last time as an employee. I
recall the first morning I entered it in that capacity. The years
have slipped away quickly, and on the whole very pleasantly.

105. PRESENTATION OF A WEDDING PRESENT
TO A YOUNGER COLLEAGUE

Gentlemen,—

We have assembled here at the beginning of our lunch-hour
for a very interesting ceremony—to congratulate our young
colleague, Mr. ——, upon his approaching marriage, to wish
him and his bride a long and happy life together, and to present him with a tangible token of our goodwill. This is a

momentous step he is taking, one that has daunted older men than he, some of whom are with us this morning; but apparently it has no terrors for Mr. ——. "Getting married, Mary," said a minister to his servant, who was giving notice for the best of all possible reasons, "is a very serious matter." "But it is not so serious as remaining single," was her reply. I am sure that is Mr. ——'s opinion. He has been going about recently as if a great weight of responsibility had been lifted from his shoulders, the overwhelming burden of bachelordom. On the whole, we think he is right. Many happy unions are represented in this gathering, and we are confident yours, Mr. ——, will add to the number. Cobbett, in his famous and unjustly neglected *Advice to Young Men*, says that among married men there exists an unacknowledged freemasonry; that because he *is* married a man is advantaged in his dealings with other benedicts. If there is such a freemasonry we shall have pleasure in admitting you to it. And now I am going to ask you, in the name of all present, and of our four travellers, whose duties forbid their presence, to accept as a wedding gift this fitted travelling-bag. It will come in handily on your approaching honeymoon, and perhaps on many subsequent happy journeys with your wife.

106. RESPONSE TO THE FOREGOING

Mr. ——, Gentlemen and Colleagues all,—

I thank you sincerely for your very handsome gift, which comes in the nick of time. I was about to buy a bag, but it would not have been nearly so handsome and expensive as this. I do thank you for your goodwill and for giving it such kindly expression. Mr. —— pulled my leg cleverly for not concealing my satisfaction at the turn my affairs have taken. Mr. —— expressed the same criticism more bluntly by saying that he would be glad when I got away, because he was sick of seeing me around "grinning like a Cheshire cat." Well, I admit that I am very happy, and it is pleasant to be assured by experienced matrimonialists that I have good cause for self-congratulation. I must not keep you from your lunches any longer. Lovers can live upon bread and cheese and kisses, but if I speak any longer there won't be left any time for even bread and cheese. I feel that I haven't thanked you enough for this princely bag.

CHAPTER XIX

IN AID OF CHARITY

107. IN FAVOUR OF ANY KIND OF CHARITY

Ladies and Gentlemen,—

There are considerably fewer charities in this country than there used to be, and I personally am glad of it. For large numbers of people to rely on charity for their very existence, as happened in the past, is an unhealthy state of affairs. It was unfair to the donors and humiliating for the recipients. Now that we have a comprehensive scheme of national insurance, many of the institutions that once depended on charity have become the responsibility of the whole community. Medical treatment and sickness and unemployment benefits are now given to all who need them. Moreover, because the scheme is a form of insurance, requiring the payment of contributions by all of us, the benefits are given not as a privilege but as a right.

In spite of these great social advances, however, I must confess that I do not think it would be beneficial if the springs of charity were to dry up altogether. When given in the proper way, charity can prove of the highest moral benefit to both donor and receiver. To the donor, the very act of giving can be ennobling; while to the recipient it may restore a flagging faith in human nature. Quite apart from the material side, an act of charity can, from its very spirit, be of inestimable value in human relationships.

But there is no danger—if it could be described as such—of the need for charity vanishing altogether. Indeed, the situation at present is quite the reverse. There is a substantial number of genuine good causes in urgent need of private assistance; and some of the most deserving of these are in greater need than they have ever been before. The fact of the matter is that while the actual number of institutions dependent on charity has decreased, the proportionate decrease in the amount of money given has been greater.

There are probably two main reasons for this. One is that those who formerly gave most generously no longer have the same amount of money at their disposal. The charitable institutions taken over by the state have to be financed by the community; and much of the money that was formerly set aside for charitable purposes is now taken off its owners in the form of taxation, and used to support the very same institutions. It would be out of place for me to express an opinion on this fact. It is sufficient to state it.

The second main reason for the falling off in subscriptions derives to some extent from the first. There is, apparently, an unfortunate belief in many quarters that, since the state now provides security for all, from the cradle to the grave, there is no longer need for any sort of charity whatever. I assure you that this is not the case; and I beg of you not to allow your judgment in this matter to be influenced by political considerations. Those good causes of which I have spoken are above politics. Whether they have been overlooked by the state, or whether the state is unable to make full provision for all of them, is beside the point. The fact is that they need your help, and that they are worthy of it.

True charity always demands a personal sacrifice. To say that you cannot afford to give is merely to furnish an added reason for giving. Consider your own circumstances; and now compare them with those of the people on whose behalf this appeal is being made. And then, I beg of you, consider again whether you cannot afford even a small subscription.

108. OPENING A BAZAAR

Ladies and Gentlemen,—

The organizers of this Bazaar have done me the great honour of asking me to declare it open, and I shall do so as shortly as possible so that I may not keep you long from making yourselves the owners of the many pretty and useful things that surround us. Those who have not actually taken part in the organization of a bazaar can have no conception of the amount of work and forethought necessary to make the function a success. The work that falls upon the stallholders during the two or three days that the bazaar is open is heavy indeed, but this is almost negligible in comparison with the long hours of preparation and organization. This parish owes a great debt of gratitude to these workers, seen and unseen. Others who have not been able to spare their time have given donations, either in money or in kind, and these also have contributed greatly to the wonderful display put before you to-day. All of us must sympathize with the object of this bazaar (*naming it*), and all of us must appreciate the efforts of the indefatigable workers, the results of whose labours you see in these well-stocked stalls; you can show your appreciation of their work in no better way than by emptying at once the stalls and your pockets, and if you go home penniless—well, so much the better.

Here you may buy almost anything you want, from a picture or an ornament to a pound of apples, and if you are persuaded by the fair stallholders and their assistants, as I am sure you easily will be persuaded, to buy something you don't want, you will have the satisfaction of knowing that your money is going where it will do good—and you can always give away your purchases.

Now I shall not detain you longer. It is with the very greatest pleasure that I declare this bazaar open.

CHAPTER XX

MISCELLANEOUS SPEECHES AND TOASTS

109. VOTE OF THANKS AFTER A PERFORMANCE BY AN AMATEUR DRAMATIC SOCIETY

Ladies and Gentlemen,—

It is a very easy task for me to get up and propose a vote of thanks to you after the performance you have given us this evening. I can tell you now that before the show began I was wondering what I could say that would be both honest and tactful if it turned out a flop. A few minutes after the curtain had gone up my fears had vanished completely. I knew then that we were in for an evening's first-class entertainment; and when the final curtain came down my pleasure was limited only by the fact that it had come to an end.

On behalf of the whole audience, which has already shown in a convincing manner that it fully shares my opinion, I wish to thank you first of all for giving us a really excellent play; secondly, for acting it in a manner that I can only call inspired; and, thirdly, for the superb staging, which speaks volumes for the work done behind the scenes.

I was going to say that the show was as good as a professional production, but I am not sure that that is a very apt comparison. For in one respect, at least, it was better than the best professional performance that the London stage can offer. You did it because you liked doing it, not for any payment: and your enthusiasm shone through the whole production, and somehow communicated itself to the audience so that we shared it with you.

In conclusion, I can only say that I wish your Society all the success in the future that it undoubtedly deserves, and I am keenly looking forward to your next production.

Thank you for a delightful evening.

110. VOTE OF THANKS AFTER A SCHOOL CONCERT

By a Parent

Ladies and Gentlemen,—

On behalf of the parents and the other members of the audience, I should like to propose a vote of thanks to all who made this concert the success that it undoubtedly has been. I will confess frankly that when my boy invited me to come and see the show, I accepted more out of a sense of duty than because I expected to be entertained. Certainly it never occurred to me that I should be treated to a show of this high standard.

I can remember when I was at school we used to put on concerts from time to time. We thoroughly enjoyed them—but I doubt if anyone else did. With your show I can safely say that you have given an evening's real pleasure to the whole audience, and we are very grateful to you for it.

It would be unfair if I were to single out any particular item for individual praise, and in any case I think it would be most difficult to do this because of the uniformly high standard of the whole programme. So I shall just say thank you, to all the performers, and to all those workers behind the scenes who helped to make the show such a triumph. They are unseen, but the results of the work are clearly visible, and I want them to know that we appreciate what they have done.

111. OPENING AN AGRICULTURAL SHOW

Speech by the Opener

Ladies and Gentlemen,—

I am convinced that no annual event is more popular in this district than this Agricultural Show, which you have done me the honour of asking me to open to-day. And it is rightly popular, for, to an agricultural and farming district such as ours, it is a function of the greatest importance. Farming has ceased to be a conservative pursuit; farmers to-day, to be successful, must adopt up-to-date methods and modern machinery, and it is shows like this, where the products of the one and examples of the other are to be seen, that are the farmer's schools; and by their help mainly he is enabled to keep abreast with the times.

There are some, I know, who think that the money spent on Agricultural Shows, and in particular the prize money,[1] could be devoted to more useful objects, but I am one of those who believe that much of the prosperity of our district has been and is due directly to these shows and to the keen competition in good farming they excite. The farmer, to carry off the prize for the best sample of wheat, for instance, has to learn how best to grow wheat; and to win the trophy for the best fat beast, he must make a science of preparing animals for the market. And unless men could come here and see the results achieved by others by better and later methods, perhaps they would not be driven by the spirit of competition and emulation to adopt those methods and incidentally to benefit themselves and agriculture in general.

Think, too, what shows and competitions have done for our stock. They have induced us to try experiments in breeding to produce the best stock for milking, for killing, for growing wool, and the best beasts of burden, and the best riding horses and hunters. They have enabled men to see together samples, if I may call them that, of various breeds of stock and to judge more or less accurately what breed or mixture of breeds will best suit their own pasturage and local conditions.

In the face of these facts, how can it be maintained that money spent on these shows is misspent?

They have another side, too. I have compared these shows to schools, and we know that almost every school has a play-ground. So have these shows, and when you have seen the exhibits and the machinery and other interesting things, you may get pleasure and amusement from watching the competitions in the ring; profit, if you are lucky, in judging the weight of the fat pig or bullock, whichever it is; and plenty of fun and jollity at the side-shows.

Now, ladies and gentlemen, I will detain you no longer. I have said, perhaps, more than enough to explain to you why it is a great pleasure to me to declare this show open as I now do.

---

[1] In giving the prizes, a few words of congratulation should be addressed to each winner.

112. THE PRESS

Proposed by the Chairman at a Dinner

Gentlemen,—

In asking you to honour the toast of The Press, I am discharging a duty which is particularly agreeable, but to that quite honest statement I must hasten to add the confession that to make a speech upon the subject at all commensurate with its importance is a task beyond my powers. The subject is so vast and appeals to us all from so many varied points of view that I suppose it would be impossible for anyone to deal adequately with even a single aspect of it in the brief limits of an after-dinner speech. The man who invented printing did much more than devise a scheme for the readier multiplication of copies of the Gospels; he found the lever to set free a force fraught with the most tremendous consequences for the whole world, of the ultimate effects of which he could not have had any adequate conception.

But it is the Newspaper Press of this country that we have more particularly in mind in proposing this toast, and we may confidently assert that it compares favourably with the Press of any other country. Nothing astonishes me so much in modern journalism as the mass of information that is daily and nightly poured forth from our newspaper offices for our amusement and edification, and in spite of the speed at which it is produced, presented with literary charm and a singularly accurate perception of the relative importance of things. With the necessity for rapid composition has come a facility of expression that is truly remarkable, and, even in the case of leading articles, which from the stress of circumstances have been written so shortly before the paper has gone to press that their authors have had no time to see a single proof, it is seldom that the most critical eye can detect evidence of the difficult conditions under which they were evolved.

Then, again, our Newspaper Press is something more than merely literary. Upon the whole it is singularly incorrupt. There are plenty of occasions when enemies of England would be only too glad to influence politically even one newspaper of standing, and there have been occasions when unlimited funds were forthcoming to produce the desired result. But I can remember no occasion when in that sense an English newspaper was found to have its price, and for that alone we cannot honour it too much.

And, lastly, there is the use our papers make of the great power they have acquired by their freedom. Surely it is a good use. Whenever there is a grievance to be remedied or a wrong to be put right, our Newspaper Press may be relied upon to step into the breach and so influence the minds of the people that the matter has to be righted through sheer force of public opinion. Individual mistakes it may be an easy matter to cite, but that collectively our Press is characterized by purity of motive, disinterestedness of purpose, and general incorruptibility I do most confidently affirm. And with equal confidence I call upon you to endorse this very imperfect eulogy of our free and national institution by drinking heartily the toast of The Press and the health of its representatives, coupled on this occasion with the name of Mr. ——.

113. REPLY TO THE FOREGOING TOAST

Mr. Chairman and Gentlemen,—

Although I am one of the humblest devotees of journalism I should be quite unworthy of the calling if I did not, at any rate, express my warm thanks for the toast you have just honoured. Believe me, however inadequately those thanks may be expressed, they are absolutely sincere. That I regard journalism as an honourable profession goes without saying, since I am devoting my own life to it, and I wish that I were better able to do justice to a subject which I have so much at heart. Regarded only as a network of commercial enterprise, our Newspaper Press is amazing. I suppose it would be impossible to compile statistics that would approximate to the truth, but the sums invested in the newspapers of the United Kingdom, and all that goes to make them up, must exceed the sums invested in any other business, apart from our great national industries. The purely commercial side of it staggers the imagination; the paper and the machinery that makes it, the type and the machinery that sets it, the ink and the machinery that prints from it; then there is the enormous advertising and distributing trade, and even then one has not begun to consider the contents of the newspapers themselves; the telegrams from all quarters of the globe, the special correspondence, the literary matter, with all its various departments of politics and literature and finance. Truly, the Press is a marvellous and intricate institution, of which no single man can do more than understand his own little department thoroughly.

The leaders in journalism to-day require qualities which would fit them for leadership in almost any profession : intelligence, courage, both moral and physical, daring, tact, quick decision, resourcefulness and sound judgment; all these attributes, and more, are needed in the service of the Press to-day. The tendency of journalism is towards literature, and it is an old saying that literature is a hard mistress, demanding much from her votaries, but there is little to grieve at in that; what's lightly won is seldom well worth having; the pre-eminence to which our Newspaper Press has attained, has been attained only by infinite pains, and that, I suppose, is why we value it so much. You have shown that you value it by your cordiality in drinking this toast, and in the names of my fellow-scribes, I thank you.

114. THE MAYOR AND CORPORATION

Mr. Chairman and Gentlemen,—

I rise to give you a toast that is of interest to all of us—the Mayor and Corporation of our town. I have often wondered why these important gentlemen do not receive more attention and notice than they do. I am perfectly aware that several times a year they are the object of the collective curse of the community when the rate collector pays his duty call, but that is not the kind of attention I mean.

How much each one of us owes to them and their work, the slightest reflection will show. Suppose they suddenly "went on strike," where should we be? You would get up in the morning and go to your bath—no water; after washing in that from your water bottle you would go down to breakfast—no electric light or gas, no bacon and eggs, or tea; you would leave your house and slip into a morass where once ran a road, you would find no bus to take you to work, and arriving finally, after many unpleasant adventures on the way, you would be dismissed for being late. In every part of our daily life, then, we feel the influences of these gentlemen and the enterprises they conduct. They watch over our comfort, our health, our very lives, and for all their work, their sacrifice of time and trouble, they get no reward.

It is, indeed, a happy thing for us that we have found men like the Mayor and his colleagues to carry on this work, men of ability and honour who take a pride in making the district an example of good government to all others. They worthily carry on the British traditions of honesty and probity in public and civic life; they are untiring in their efforts for our good; the least that we can give them is our gratitude and our thanks. Gentlemen, I give you the toast of the Mayor and Corporation.

115. REPLY TO THE FOREGOING TOAST

Mr. Chairman and Gentlemen,—

Before I heard Mr. —— propose the toast to which you have just given so warm and kindly a reception, my colleagues and I were ignorant of our real importance; I see now that we shall have to get into the way of regarding ourselves as public benefactors.

Seriously, I may say this : that we do our best for the people who have shown their confidence in us by putting us in our present positions, and we do really try to give them as little reason as possible for cursing us when our rate collector reminds them of our existence.

We have many enterprises to conduct, many departments to control, and if, as I think is the fact, things go fairly smoothly as a rule, your thanks are due rather to the capable and efficient staff which more directly manages our various departments than to us. For our own parts, the work is a labour of love, it interests us and we take much pride in our municipality. For my colleagues and myself, I thank you very much for the kind way in which this toast has been proposed and received.

116. THE FIRE BRIGADE

Proposed at a Municipal or other Dinner

Gentlemen,—

I have been called upon to propose a toast to our Fire Brigade, which from the childhood days when our greatest delight was to see the engines streaming past in response to a call, has always held a place in our hearts. Of the important duties which it so ably performs, it is only necessary for me to say a few words. Although, let us hope, there is no one present to-night who has had occasion to enlist its help, I do not think anybody will dispute that of all branches of the municipal service, none deserves greater credit or more encouragement than the Fire Brigade. We are well aware of the distress and suffering that may result from an outbreak of fire, and it is upon the resource and energy of our Brigade that security of life and property to a large extent depends. And, gentlemen, I may safely say that whenever the services of our firemen have been requisitioned, they have fulfilled their arduous duties most efficiently and have justified the confidence placed in them. We must not, however, in praising the efficiency of the Brigade, overlook the important factors that have contributed to its splendid organization and discipline, with which we have for so long associated the name of our worthy and respected guest, ——, to whose untiring efforts in this direction the highest credit should be paid. It is to their undaunted courage and constant readiness to face danger when life and property are at stake, that the popularity and respect that the Fire Brigade have gained are due, and I have the greatest pleasure in asking you to drink to the welfare of the men of the Fire Brigade.

117. REPLY TO THE FOREGOING TOAST

By the Chief Officer of the Fire Brigade

Mr. —— and Gentlemen,—

I have to thank the proposer of the toast for the too flattering way in which he spoke of the Fire Brigade, and you for the very friendly reception you gave to his remarks. Still, I can assure you that your appreciation of the efforts of the Brigade will greatly encourage the men, and help them to maintain the present standard of efficiency. Without egotism, I may truly say that the members of the Brigade do not spare themselves. It would be absurd to declare that they love their work, but they recognize that it is necessary to the security of the community, and therefore they undertake it with a desire to do it thoroughly. The work is exacting, responsible, and dangerous, and demands pluck, presence of mind, and almost abnormal activity. These qualities, I believe, characterize the present staff, and they will always be at the disposal of our townsfolk whenever occasion for their display unfortunately arrives. These social gatherings offer an agreeable relief to my duties, and it has afforded me sincere pleasure to know that you have not forgotten the arduous services of your Fire Brigade. Gentlemen, I thank you.

118. THE POLICE FORCE

Proposed at a Municipal or other Dinner

Mr. Chairman and Gentlemen,—

We are all law-abiding citizens here—at least, I hope so—and the toast it is my pleasant duty to propose is one that cannot but commend itself to law-abiding citizens—it is that of the Police Force.

Candidly, gentlemen, when I reflect how much of our peace and ease of mind is due to the "Man in Blue," I shudder to think what would be our plight if he and his uniform were suddenly to desert our streets. Imagine the horrible contingency of a police strike, with Bill Sikes and all his friends free to work their will on our hapless selves. But I must not introduce horrors to spoil the harmony of the evening; this I shall say, that few of us could be here enjoying our dinner with minds free of care and anxiety did we not know that our homes are under the constable's vigilant supervision! Whether he be indulging in a little nocturnal flirtation with Mary Jane, or holding up the traffic to enable a timid old lady to cross a busy street, or taking under his paternal care the small child "found wandering," or fulfilling sterner functions in "running in" Bill Sikes, Robert carries out his part with characteristic conscientiousness. In these days of industrial unrest our police have most difficult duties to perform—duties demanding the exercise of great tact and discretion. We are delighted to know that our police have stood the test, and have dispelled many an ugly temper by their invariable humour. Their sound common sense has in many cases averted a crisis which threatened to be very serious. Let us then, gentlemen, show our appreciation of their services by raising our glasses in honour of "The Force." To give point to our praise, I ask you to associate with the toast the name of Inspector ——, and to wish him and his colleagues long life, happiness, and prosperity.

119. REPLY TO THE FOREGOING TOAST

Mr. ——, and Gentlemen,—

I am quite taken aback by the honour you have so unexpectedly done me. I came here to enjoy myself, to spend a pleasant evening among you, and the last thing I thought I should be required to do was to make a speech. But I must at all events thank the proposer for his kindly and humorous remarks, and the company for their hearty acceptance of them. It is nice to know that the police force have earned the friendly appreciation of their fellow-townsmen. There is, I believe, good authority for the notion that "a policeman's lot is not a happy one." Sir William Gilbert perhaps spoke from a personal experience that may not have been wholly agreeable, or, like King David, he may have uttered his opinion "in haste." For if I were to take him seriously I fear I should have to qualify his remarks with a very large pinch of salt. We know what our duties are and are always ready to take the rough with the smooth. Every man of us has gone through a prolonged course of training, and that enables us to face our daily or nightly round without giving undue thought to the troubles and difficulties that may be in store for us. We know what is expected of us, and it is our constant aim and endeavour to render as good an account of ourselves as we can. Gentlemen, for your considerate and valued approval I thank you.

120. A SCHOOL TREAT

By the Leader of the Excursion

Ladies and Gentlemen,—

Before we leave this place where we have all spent such a delightful day, I want you to give three cheers for Mr. ——, by whose courtesy and kindness we have been enabled to enjoy ourselves so much. He is not present with us now, but I hope he will understand how fully we appreciate his kindness in permitting us to come here and picnic and enjoy ourselves, as we have all done to-day. We are glad to think there has been no damage done, and that you have all, boys and girls, behaved well and had a thoroughly good time. Such good conduct will, no doubt, influence Mr. ——, if we again wish to spend an afternoon in his beautiful park. By giving him a hearty cheer I hope you will tell him how much we all appreciate his kindness. I won't ask you to wish him many returns of *this* day; still let us wish him long life and prosperity. Now, boys and girls, three cheers for Mr. ——.

Now, there is another thing—and I hope you are not all

hoarse after those cheers, because I may want some more before I have done. There are some ladies and gentlemen present who have, at some inconvenience, but very willingly, come down with us to-day to assist us in our sports, and to make things go smoothly. They have also subscribed very liberally for the prizes you have won, and in many other ways have helped us all to enjoy ourselves. We owe them a vote of thanks, and I am sure you will all unite with me in thanking our visitors very heartily for what they have done, and for the kind way they have assisted us to-day. Now then, all together—three cheers for the Visitors!

121. A SCHOOL "SPORTS"

Distribution of Prizes

Ladies and Gentlemen,—

I have been requested to give away the prizes this afternoon, and I have very great pleasure in doing so, particularly as I have watched the sports with great interest, and feel that the winners thoroughly deserve them.

The time has long since gone by when people, and especially parents, thought that no other lessons were to be learnt in school than the lessons of the class-room, and nowadays we recognize that, besides improving a boy's physical development and health, the playing fields teach him many things that he cannot get from books alone. Games teach you how to "keep a stiff upper lip" when you are beaten, not to become "swollen headed" with success, and above all to keep on trying, whether at work or at play. For our whole life is a race—a struggle in which the weakest will fall behind. There is so much competition nowadays in everything that unless a man is prepared to put every ounce of his energy into his work he cannot hope to reach the top of the ladder of success. So I hope all you young people who hear me will remember how you have gained your prizes—viz., by doing your best. Now, if you carry this idea out in your lives generally, and do your best—not *the* very best, of course, for others may beat you, but your best according to your abilities and opportunities—you will be astonished how quickly you will come to the front. And you who are beaten to-day, remember that there are other races to win and that in the long run there is always a reward for the man who perseveres and is a "trier."

> "If what shone afar so grand
>   Turn to nothing in your hand,
>   On again, the merit lies
>   In the striving, not the prize."

But no man can be strong in combat or running unless his heart is right, and in the right order for work. So in moral, as well as in physical exercises, the *heart* must be right.

I will not longer detain you. Remember, if you can, my advice. Do your best, and leave the result and the verdict to the Judge. Now, if you please, I will hand the prizes to the successful competitors.[1]

122. THE OLD SCHOOL

Mr. Chairman,—

There can be few honours more pleasing to an old boy than to be called upon to propose the health and prosperity of his old school.

Having been an old boy in the eyes of the school for the last thirty years, I fear that I am rapidly becoming an old boy in the eyes of that larger school—the world. And I ask myself to-night, "Can I be the same old boy as the youth who thirty years ago was let loose upon an unoffending and unsuspecting world? Can it be that to-night I have dined with and even spoken to Captains and Prefects, when there was a time when I dare not even have looked? Is it true that I could not answer the simplest question of Latin Grammar and should be floored by a Maths. test that would be simplicity itself to the junior school dunce?" Yes, Mr. Chairman, I fear it is too true, yet altered, disfigured and degenerate as I no doubt am, I know that there still burns in me something of the old school spirit.

Some of us may not have learnt much at school, but we had the best possible Masters—some of them I am delighted to see here to-night. They taught us what was really worth knowing, and made us want to know it; they also put us in the right path of learning it. They showed us what the real spirit of the school was—the spirit which has made great men in the past and has made us, if not great, yet proud of our association with it. At the Old School we were taught much more than Latin, French and Arithmetic. We were taught "how to play the game"; we

[1] In giving the prizes, a few words of congratulation should be addressed to each winner

were taught how to control our tempers; we were taught to obey, so that later we might command. Yes, not only have we to thank our Old School for offering us a good knowledge of the "classics" or of "modern" subjects, according to the "side" we took up, but it endeavoured to send us out into the world with the will and the training to be of some use to our country in particular and to the world in general.

After so many years school friends and associates get scattered. Their interests diverge; some become great in commerce or profession, some labour for the State at home and abroad, and necessarily some fall by the wayside; but of this I am sure, that each one is proud of being an Old —— and wishes he had been worthier of that grand old *Alma Mater* which gave him his first chance.

Gentlemen, the toast is "The Old School."

THE PERSONAL APPLICATION OF TITLES

THE colloquial application of titles differs materially from the written form.

A British duke and duchess are normally addressed as "Your Grace."

A British marquis is addressed colloquially as "Lord B.," not as "Marquis," and a marchioness as "Lady B." The correct formal mode of address is "My Lord" and "My Lady." This rule applies generally to other members of the peerage below the rank of duke and duchess.

A duke's eldest son and his wife will be addressed by social acquaintances as "Lord B." and "Lady B."; as "My Lord" and "My Lady" by all others.

The younger son of a duke is addressed as "Lord John A." or "Lord Charles A." by acquaintances, and as "My Lord" by others. Their immediate friends would address them by their title and Christian names, as "Lord John" and "Lord Charles," their wives being generally addressed as "Lady John" and "Lady Charles."

The daughters of a duke are addressed as "Lady Mary A." or "Lady Elizabeth B." by social acquaintances; as "Lady Mary" or "Lady Elizabeth" by those intimate with them; as "My Lady" by others.

The eldest son of a marquis is addressed as "Lord A." by

acquaintances, and as "My Lord" by others; his wife as "Lady A." or "My Lady."

These rules are followed in the case of the sons of all members of the peerage, the sons' wives, and the daughters of all members of the peerage. The younger sons of earls, as also the eldest and younger sons of viscounts and barons, bear the courtesy title of "Honourable." The daughters of viscounts and barons also bear the courtesy title of "Honourable." This title should never be used personally in speaking: "The Honourable Roderick B.," "The Honourable Mrs. Roderick B.," and "The Honourable Grace B." would be styled "Mr., Mrs. or Miss Grace B."

Baronets are addressed by their full title and surname as "Sir John B." by acquaintances, by their titles and Christian names by others. Their wives are addressed by acquaintances as "Lady B." or "Lady C." according to the surname of their husbands. Thus "Sir John B.'s" wife should be addressed as "Lady B.," not as "Lady John B."; to do so would be to give her the rank of the wife of a younger son of a duke. Others address her as "My Lady."